Derham Groves is a Melbourne-based architect and pop-culture historian. He holds a Bachelor of Architecture from Deakin University, a Master of Architecture from the Royal Melbourne Institute of Technology, and a Doctor of Philosophy from the University of Minnesota. His research interests include Chinese temples in Australia, the world of Sherlock Holmes, and Australian folk art and design. *Mail Art: The Do-It-Yourself Letterbox from Workshop to Gatepost* is his third book.

Mail Art

The Do-It-Yourself Letterbox from Workshop to Gatepost

Derham Groves

HALE
& IREMONGER

For Ping and Huey

10 9 8 7 6 5 4 3 2 1

Typeset by
DOCUPRO, Sydney

Printed and bound by
Southwood Press Pty Ltd
80–92 Chapel Street, Marrickville NSW 2204

For the publisher
Hale & Iremonger Pty Ltd
PO Box 205, Alexandria NSW 2015

National Library of Australia
Cataloguing-in-Publication entry:

Groves, Derham
Mail art: the do-it-yourself letterbox from workshop to gatepost.

Bibliography.
Includes index.

ISBN 0 86806 645 1

1. Mailboxes—Social aspects—Australia. I. Title

392.360994

This project has been assisted by the Commonwealth Government through the Australia Council, its art funding and advisory body.

Contents

Acknowledgements   7
Preface   9

 I The Do-It-Yourself Phenomenon
    1   Backyard Inventors and Madcap Inventions   23
    2   Home Workshop as Playhouse   39

II The Letterbox Phenomenon
    3   The Letterbox that Jerry Built   61
    4   Learning from Letterboxes   94

Select Bibliography   109
Index   119

Acknowledgements

I wish to thank the following people for helping me in various ways with this book: Professor Karal Ann Marling, my pop culture 'guru' from the Department of Art History at the University of Minnesota, for her encouragement throughout; Michael Jorgensen, architect and crime novelist extraordinaire, John Arnold, my drinking-mate from the National Centre for Australian Studies (NCAS) at Monash University, and Robert Littlewood, raconteur and private press publisher, for their valuable comments and suggestions; the students of the Department of Architecture and Design at the Royal Melbourne Institute of Technology (RMIT), especially Lucy Brylski, Maria Casablanca, Azian Huzairi, Julia Lam, Nick Peraic, Peter Pezos, Deborah Ross, Phillip Rowe, John Scaramuzzino, Sam Stephens and Martin Zweep, for their lively discussions and hard work; Roger Fay, the editor of *Exedra*, and Stephen Banham, the editor of *Qwerty*, for publishing some of my work along the way; Jennifer Nugent from Australia Post (Victoria), Professor Chris Ryan from the Key Centre for Design at RMIT and Professor Peter Spearritt from NCAS, for their assistance with the exhibition, 'Letterboxes'; Clark Barrett, Peter D. Cole, John Graham, Louise Lovett, Helmut Lueckenhausen, Maggie McCormick, Mary Newsome, Andrew Reed, Alex Selenitsch, Joy Smith, Akira Takizawa (another drinking-mate) and David Wong for participating in this exhibition; Associate Professor

Judy Stone Nunneley and the printmaking students from the Minneapolis College of Art and Design, especially Ann Danielson and Rosemary Riskin, for participating in the exhibition, 'Life in a Letterbox'; Professor Rick Asher from the Department of Art History at the University of Minnesota and Associate Professors Richard Fooks and Sand Helsel from the Department of Architecture and Design at RMIT, for oiling the wheels of bureaucracy; Rhonda Black and Bert Hingley, my publishers at Hale & Iremonger, for their show of faith and some amusing faxes; and last but not least, Khoo Ping Tiang and Huey Groves for their unflagging love and support.

Derham Groves
Brunswick West
April 1998

Preface

We shall not cease from exploration
And the end of all our exploring
Will be to arrive where we started
And know the place for the first time.

'Little Gidding', T.S. Eliot

I first became interested in Australian, contemporary, vernacular design during the 1970s, while studying architecture at Deakin University in country Victoria. Not very much had been written on this subject—or at least, not very much which was positive. Many people regarded *The Australian Ugliness* (1960), the extremely negative critique of the Australian suburbs by the Australian architect and author, Robin Boyd, as the final word on the subject. However, I wanted to look at things from a very different point of view.

Ever since adolescence, I have been an admirer of Sir Arthur Conan Doyle's celebrated sleuth, Sherlock Holmes. Like the great detective's friend and biographer, Dr John H. Watson, I was also very impressed with Holmes's ability to deduce astounding facts from seemingly commonplace details. No hocus-pocus was involved. As Holmes told Watson: 'You know my method. It is founded on the observance of trifles.' Holmes gives a good demonstration of his extraordinary powers in

'The Adventure of the Blue Carbuncle' (1891). After closely examining 'a very seedy hard felt hat', he is able to say the following things about its owner, a complete stranger:

> That the man was highly intellectual is of course obvious upon the face of it, and also that he was fairly well-to-do within the last three years, although he has now fallen upon evil days. He had foresight, but has less now than formerly, pointing to a moral retrogression, which, when taken with the decline of his fortunes, seems to indicate some evil influence, probably drink, at work upon him. This may account also for the obvious fact that his wife has ceased to love him.

I wanted to look at the Australian suburbs through the eyes of Sherlock Holmes. This is not as silly as it sounds. Several very distinguished scholars have either consciously or unconsciously also adopted Holmes's methods of investigation. For example, the British ethnographer, Dr Alfred C. Haddon, wrote:

Actors Christopher Plummer and Thorley Walters as Sherlock Holmes and Dr Watson. The methods of the Great Detective may also be applied to the study of the Australian suburbs.

In ethnology, as in other sciences, nothing is too insignificant to receive attention. Indeed, it is a matter of common experience among scientific men that apparently trivial objects have an interest and importance that are by no means commensurate with the estimation in which they are ordinarily held.

The American landscape theorist, John Brinckerhoff Jackson, expresses a similar viewpoint in his book, *Discovering the Vernacular Landscape* (1984):

Over and over again I have said that the commonplace aspects of the contemporary landscape, the streets and houses and fields and places of work, could teach us a great deal not only about American history and American society but about ourselves and how we relate to the world. It is a matter of learning how to see.

The great detective was also a source of inspiration for the English designer, Gordon Russell. In his autobiography, *Designer's Trade* (1968), Russell said:

The discovery of Sherlock Holmes at about this time [1911] was a memorable one. Not only were the stories first-rate entertainment but they taught me to try to deduce what happened from clues painstakingly observed and tracked down. This has been a

A letterbox in the form of a house in the Geelong suburb of Belmont.

source of interest which has grown with the years, of great value
to a designer.

Looking around the suburbs of Geelong, my home town, one
of the first things I observed was an incredible variety of
do-it-yourself letterboxes or mailboxes, including ones like tree
stumps, miniature houses, fire alarms, and wine barrels. I
doubt whether Robin Boyd would have approved of them,
although, surprisingly, he did not discuss do-it-yourself
letterboxes in *The Australian Ugliness*. However, he may have
had them in mind when he disapprovingly wrote:

> The symbol or the image, the miniature of the new aspiration,
> is applied to the old thing in the hope that it will tinge the whole
> thing with new colour. And, to unalerted eyes, indeed a feature
> can succeed in suffusing the whole of the thing to which it
> adheres. The ordinary wigwam [i.e. the house?] becomes an
> object of awe when a totem [i.e. a do-it-yourself letterbox?] is
> added.

But these delightful, do-it-yourself letterboxes inspired me to
mount a modest exhibition at Deakin University in 1977. I
made a cardboard model of a typical suburban house, about
the size of a large doll's house, and projected slides of several
do-it-yourself letterboxes onto one of its windows. While this
highlighted an interesting suburban phenomenon, I regret to
say that it did very little else. The novelty of the subject was
too overwhelming—so much for my great powers of deduction!

I did not pursue the subject of do-it-yourself letterboxes
any further until about ten years later, when I was studying
for a Master of Architecture degree at the Royal Melbourne
Institue of Technology (RMIT) in Melbourne. For my Master's
thesis, I compared 'feng–shui' (wind–water), the Chinese
system of divination used to find auspicious sites for buildings
and graves, with various Western building ceremonies, such as
ground-breaking and foundation-stone ceremonies. I concluded
that both ceremonial systems had a lot in common, and as a
result of this work my interest in do-it-yourself letterboxes was
rekindled.

I could see similarities between some Australian do-it-yourself letterboxes and some Chinese talismans, used to create
good feng–shui. For example, in Imperial China, palaces and

temples were protected from fire by dragonlike roof decorations, 'chi-wen'. In East Malaysia, shop-houses are sometimes protected from malign forces by various charms, including daggers, fans, mirrors, and scissors, placed above doors and windows. And in Taiwan, farm houses are sometimes protected from evil spirits by symbolic forts (bamboo stakes at the four corners of the house), manned by supernatural soldiers.

In Australia, letterboxes are usually located on the street boundary, either next to the driveway or the garden gate. It appeared to me that some people had turned their do-it-yourself letterboxes into Chinese-style protective charms. The letterbox like a missile-launcher looked as though it was meant to deter burglars, and the letterboxes like fire alarms, fire extinguishers and fire hydrants looked as though they were meant to prevent fire. Perhaps Australian culture was more 'spiritual' than I had thought it was.

I began collecting slides of as many do-it-yourself letterboxes as I could. By now I was teaching architecture at RMIT. My students found interesting letterboxes for me. I wrote to suburban post offices, asking the local 'posties' (letter carriers) if there were any unusual letterboxes on their rounds. And I kept my eyes open for do-it-yourself letterboxes on my

A letterbox which appears to be a cross between Abraham Lincoln and Thomas the Tank Engine near Bright, Victoria.

travels interstate and overseas—in particular, in North America. However, it seems that nowhere else in the world do people express themselves through their letterboxes with quite so much fervour and passion as do Australians, and especially Melburnians.

Despite this, however, do-it-yourself letterboxes are such an integral part of the Australian landscape that they are often taken for granted. Therefore it is hardly surprising that very little has been written about them: only a handful of articles and two books. *Australian Country Mail Boxes* (1972) by Hans J. Breitgraf, a German diplomat, and *Dinkum Aussie Mail Boxes: Rural Art Treasures of Australia* (1982) by Alan Egar, an Australian journalist.

Unfortunately, both Breitgraf and Egar simply deal with the subject in a superficial way, leaving many important questions unanswered. For example, they do not explain why so many people go to the trouble of making such extraordinary letterboxes as the ones shown in their books. In addition, neither author considers do-it-yourself letterboxes in the Australian suburbs. Breitgraf suggests a reason for this curious omission:

> People who live near a post office, whether this is in a city, town or village, have their mail delivered by postmen who put it in a 'letterbox'. Though these letterboxes are mostly well designed and attractive to the eye, they are nearly always mass-produced and not do-it-yourself, and for that reason they are not included in this survey.

Breitgraf is wrong, however, as my research clearly shows: suburban letterboxes are not 'nearly always mass-produced', as he claimed, but are often handmade. However, had Breitgraf been writing before World War II, his statement may well have been correct, because it appears that suburban do-it-yourself letterboxes were principally a post-war phenomenon. Let me briefly explain the events that led to this occurrence.

In Australia, following World War II, a severe housing shortage, aggravated by a lack of manpower and materials, led many people to build their own homes and carry out their own home improvements and repairs. As the post-war do-it-yourself movement gained momentum, increasing numbers of how-to-do-it books and magazines, easy-to-use home decorating products and portable power tools were developed especially for do-it-yourselfers.

At the same time, the increasingly push-button, sedentary nature of work deprived men of the invigorating physicality of manual labour. As a result, many men saw themselves as merely dispensable automatons at the factory or the office. To compensate for the lack of stimulation at work, they often took up physically demanding hobbies, like carpentry.

In the course of re-fashioning their homes to reflect their personal tastes, do-it-yourselfers produced highly individual artefacts, such as bird houses, doghouses, garden ornaments, and, of course, letterboxes. Certainly, making a letterbox was an ideal do-it-yourself project. It was an extremely useful thing—after all, practically every house needed one. It required only a modest amount of materials, which could have been almost anything, even junk, so it did not cost very much. And it was a relatively quick and simple job, although it could still challenge a do-it-yourselfer's skill, imagination and creativity, because the 'secondary' functions of a letterbox as a boundary

A flower pot holder in the Melbourne suburb of Brunswick gained a new lease on life as a letterbox holder.
A letterbox made from rocks in the Melbourne suburb of North Balwyn appears to almost defy gravity.

marker and a symbol of home were often far more important than its 'primary' function as a container for the mail.

The do-it-yourself movement and letterboxes were also linked by Australia's isolation from the rest of the world. According to the Australian historian and journalist, C.E.W. Bean, this had produced a country of do-it-yourselfers:

> It is still a quality of the Australian that he can make something out of nothing . . . he has had to do without the best things; because they don't exist there, so he has made the next best do; and when even these are not to hand, he has manufactured them out of things which one would have thought it impossible to turn to any use at all.

Furthermore, I believe that Australia's isolation was also partly responsible for this country's preoccupation with letterboxes, because as receptacles for the mail they helped to bring people closer together.

Unfortunately, the history of Australian letterboxes has been poorly documented. However, a few items indicate that do-it-yourself letterboxes were very popular in the Australian suburbs after World War II. The author of 'Is Your Number Showing?' (1948) wrote: 'We have recently noticed the trend in newly built houses towards fancy letterboxes which, instead of being fixed on the inner side of the fence, stand up on a post of their own, somewhat after the manner of a dovecote.'

In 'Post Taste' (1948), Ronald Price featured a letterbox surmounted by a mail coach silhouette, a letterbox 'moulded on the lines of a Maori hut', and a letterbox like 'a tiny replica of a house'. Price said:

> Letterboxes can play quite an important part in adding to the personality of homes. With the popularity of brick fences the hole-in-the-pillar letterbox has become standard equipment for new houses, but none has the charm of the independent box— especially an original one in keeping with the house and garden.

In *The Walls Around Us* (1962), Robin Boyd illustrated the concept of 'suburban style' with his own sketches of six 'rather typical Australian houses', dating from the 1880s to the 1950s. Significantly, a do-it-yourself letterbox appears only in front of the 1950s house, strongly suggesting that this type of letterbox was a common feature after the war, but not before.

Six 'rather typical Australian houses' dating from the 1880s (*top left-hand corner*) to the 1950s (*bottom right-hand corner*) drawn by Robin Boyd. Note the do-it-yourself letterbox in front of the 1950s house.

This do-it-yourself letterbox also suggests that 'contemporary [architecture] lent itself to the do-it-yourself movement in and around the home'.

Furthermore, there is solid, anecdotal evidence to suggest that suburban do-it-yourself letterboxes were principally a post-war phenomenon. Take Jeff Maynard's charming short story, 'The Letterbox War of Kamarooka Street' (1991), for example, which is set during the 1950s in the Melbourne suburb of Sunshine. On their way to school, the author and his friend, Clarry Wilson, stop to admire a new do-it-yourself letterbox at number 6 Kamarooka Street: 'It was made of wood, painted blue, with a small wooden chimney and an A-shaped roof open at the front and the back so that it could accept the daily paper. Around the sides were painted doors and windows and the windows even had painted curtains.' This letterbox inadvertently starts the letterbox war of Kamarooka Street, with one resident trying to creatively outdo the others. During the months ahead, the delighted schoolboys discover several more do-it-yourself letterboxes shaped like miniature houses, including one in the style of a Swiss chalet, a medieval castle, an aircraft hangar, and a Dutch windmill. While the story is fiction, it is based on Maynard's childhood memories of post-war Sunshine.

Mail Art: The Do-It-Yourself Letterbox from Workshop to Gatepost is divided into two parts. Part I, 'The Do-It-Yourself Phenomenon', consists of two chapters. In Chapter 1, 'Backyard Inventors and Madcap Inventions', I describe several types of post-war do-it-yourselfers, ranging from owner–builders to hopeless handymen, who were responsible for the first batch of do-it-yourself letterboxes in the Australian suburbs. I also discuss some reasons why do-it-yourself activities were so popular in Australia and the United States during the 1950s. It is important to consider the influence of the United States because, after World War II, Australia increasingly followed this country's lead in most things, including the do-it-yourself movement. As Robin Boyd wrote:

> It is the American now who comes from Mecca. The comparative similarities between Australia and America socially, historically and in size, are clear. At times like the gold rush period a century ago when many from California transferred to the Australian diggings, and the Second World War when many American soldiers were based in Australia, a strong feeling of identification with the United States has been apparent.

In Chapter 2, 'Home Workshop as Playhouse', I examine some of the roles which home workshops played during their heyday, the 1950s. These include being a work place, a playhouse and a fallout shelter. Given that mostly men were interested in do-it-yourself pastimes like carpentry, it is not surprising that home workshops were male strongholds, and that letterbox-making was a male-dominated activity. A number of scholars have recently investigated the effects of gender on post-war domestic architecture. However, more work seems to have been done on the woman's domain than on the man's. To some extent, my research into home workshops and do-it-yourself letterboxes addresses this apparent imbalance.

It is possible to gain an interesting insight into do-it-yourself letterboxes by looking at home workshops. As small, domestic, garden structures, both help to define 'front' and 'back' in the home. The letterbox is an important element—if not the main focus—of the front garden, while the home workshop, especially one in the form of a shed, is an important element of the backyard. Accordingly, an attention-grabbing do-it-yourself letterbox corresponds with the showy nature of the front garden, while a humble looking shed reflects the casual character of the backyard.

Part II, 'The Letterbox Phenomenon', also consists of two chapters. In Chapter 3, 'The Letterbox that Jerry Built', I examine the iconography of Australian do-it-yourself letterboxes. I discuss some of the important cultural roles they play, including being a vehicle of personal creativity, a symbol of home, and target of vandalism. By the same token, I also describe their function as silent sentinels and guardians of gates. I point out some parallels between roadside architecture and do-it-yourself letterboxes, especially those which reflect their owners' occupations and hobbies. And I reflect on how all of this might change if the design of letterboxes is standardised at some time in the future, like it was in the United States.

In Chapter 4, 'Learning from Letterboxes', I describe several seminars and exhibitions I have organised as an architect and academic, which have helped me to develop some of my theories about do-it-yourself letterboxes. One important thing which this work has enabled me to do is view a variety of processes for designing and making do-it-yourself letterboxes. It has also highlighted some interesting distinctions between fine art and folk art.

PART I

The Do-It-Yourself Phenomenon

1   Backyard Inventors and Madcap Inventions

The do-it-yourself decade

The 1950s might well be called the do-it-yourself decade. Consider the following facts and figures from the United States (merely a sample of those quoted with pride in 1950s how-to-do-it magazines to illustrate what was then the latest trend). In 1952, do-it-yourselfers built either entirely or in part more than a quarter of a million, or one in four, new houses. In 1953, a survey revealed there were eleven million home workshops in the United States. During the same year, do-it-yourselfers spent a total of $6,000,000,000 on 'everything from thumbtacks to pre-cut building materials all for their homes'. Indeed, as do-it-yourself activities grew in popularity, an increasing number of easy-to-use products were developed, such as dripless paint and pre-pasted wallpaper. The phenomenal growth of the do-it-yourself industry could be measured by the sales of power tools. Americans bought power tools worth a total of $40,000,000 in 1950, more than double this amount in 1952, and more than double this amount again in 1955.

The post-war do-it-yourself movement also took Australia by storm. The Australian do-it-yourself commentator, Wally Driscoll, claimed that 'the adaptable Australian is applying do-it-yourself even more thoroughly than his American cousin'. Once again, the growth of the do-it-yourself industry could be measured in terms of power tools. In 1949, almost a quarter of a million electric motors for power tools were produced in Australia. Only three years later, the number produced had more than doubled.

The do-it-yourself movement was a mixed blessing for professional tradesmen. It threatened the livelihood of some, like those in the painting and decorating industry, but created work for others. In an article on the do-it-yourself movement in the United States, J. Paul Taylor wrote:

> At the outset of the trend, many unions and trade groups took a dim view of the development, but now most feel that do-it-yourself suggestion actually increases the amount of work to be done since many jobs would never be started except on a do-it-yourself basis, jobs which often require professional help before completion.

Discovering things

During the 1950s, almost any magazine or newspaper worth its salt published straightforward articles on design, building construction, interior decoration, and home repairs. Sometimes these were later published as books, such as the do-it-yourselfer's 'bible', the *New Australian Home Carpentry Illustrated* (n.d.) by Alex Smith. This book contained over one hundred and seventy informative articles, ranging from selecting a kit of tools to building a house, which had been originally published in the *Australian Home Beautiful*.

The post-war do-it-yourself movement 'transformed' mere homemaking magazines into how-to-do-it magazines. In 1954, the *Australian Home Beautiful*, first published in 1925, gained the subtitle, 'Australia's How-To-Do-It Magazine'. American how-to-do-it magazines, such as *Popular Mechanics* and *Popular Science*, were also read widely in Australia. As the most comprehensive sources of do-it-yourself information, the sales of magazines like these soared in the 1950s. I shall quote freely from post-war how-to-do-it magazines, both from Australia and the United States, to try to capture the mood of the era.

Another popular source of do-it-yourself information was television. According to J. Paul Taylor, the do-it-yourself movement and television were 'partners' because a TV show which featured do-it-yourself activities was 'shown at the scene of the proposed activity, in the home'. In the United States, this was evident from the success of the TV show, 'Walt's Workshop'. Each week, the show's host, the former carpentry teacher, Walter Durbahn, demonstrated everything from 'making parakeet paraphernalia to fitting and hanging a door'.

In Australia, one of the first TV shows to feature do-it-yourself activities was the 'House & Garden Magazine Show' (1958). It was hosted by 'a modern young couple, Mr and Mrs Sydney' (played by TV personalities Brian Henderson and Valerie Cooney), who had 'just bought a house (not a new one—they couldn't afford it), and now they're starting from scratch, modernising, re-decorating and later, planning a garden'. This also described most of the show's viewers. The show featured the ideas put forward each month in the homemaking magazine, *Australian House & Garden*. This was clever because, before the invention of the home video recorder, it was much easier for somebody trying to follow a series of instructions to read (and re-read) a magazine article, rather than watch a TV show.

On the other hand, watching television distracted some people from do-it-yourself activities. In 1953, the American magazine, *Collier's*, published a cartoon showing a woman holding a broken insect screen and blocking her husband's view of the television set. Referring to the broken insect screen, the woman said to her husband: 'I think it's time you gave a little of your attention to these forty-two-inch screens.'

Jacks of all trades

Men were often judged as men on the basis of their do-it-yourself skills. As one do-it-yourself expert pointed out: 'What mother does not thank the boy who can fix her ironing cord and set in an extra shelf? And what wife does not thank the husband who can put new slats into the baby's play-pen and build an extra corner cupboard?'

On the other hand, according to A.E. Mander, author of *The Making of the Australians* (1958), people 'still have some small measure of disdain for the electician who can't knock up a packing case or lay a concrete path . . . for the university professor who can't paint his own ceiling or mend a grandfather clock; for the doctor who can't effect running repairs, not only to his patients, but to his car!'

In 'You Can Become a *Handy* Handyman' (1951), Robinson Murray suggested nine basic rules to help men acquire do-it-yourself skills which their friends would envy and their wives would admire: Take your time. Be audacious. Ask questions. Seek expert instruction. Hoard literature. Get plans of projects. Choose tools carefully. Take care of your tools. Let power tools work for you.

Boys were expected to acquire these skills either at school or at home. Ideally, this involved more than merely making fruit baskets, milk-bottle holders, pencil boxes, and so on. More importantly, it was one means by which a boy could learn 'methods of thinking, planning and working that will stick with him as long as he lives', according to the author of 'Teach Your Child to Work with Tools' (1954). He advised the fathers of boys that 'lessons in good workmanship you teach your boy now will, as he grows older, help him think in terms of "do it right" in many other matters than woodworking'.

Women were encouraged to take an interest in carpentry— albeit for reasons that most people would find utterly objectionable today. The author of the above article, for example, suggested that 'a young daughter who learns early to appreciate good craftsmanship may end up someday as an all-the-better wife for some handyman-around-the-house'. Many women did, indeed, play a supportive role. The wives of the members of the Thursday Night Club, a group of amateur woodworkers from Minneapolis in the United States, proudly made '"heroes" out of their handymen husbands by smoothing over their mistakes with wood putty'.

But some women wanted to do more than merely 'play second fiddle'. Mary Hardy of Melbourne was a good example. An article in the *Australian Home Beautiful* (1959), which would be viewed as unacceptably patronising today, said she had 'crowded plenty of achievements into her life—most of them in spheres generally reserved for men'. She could expertly operate a Shopsmith, a multi-purpose power tool consisting of a circular saw, a drill press, a lathe, and a disc sander. During her spare time, she had renovated her house and made prize-winning toys for her nephews and nieces.

The house that Jack built

Hardly any houses were built in Australia during World War II, which meant that approximately four hundred thousand new houses were urgently needed at the war's end. An Australian short film, *The City* (1957), looked at this problem through the eyes of Kathie (played by Joan Landor) and Ted (played by Brian Vicery), a young couple who felt they were unable to marry because of the shortage of houses.

While on her way to work, Kathie scanned 'Houses For Sale' in the newspaper. As she read the prices she said to herself in despair: 'Even if you crossed off the noughts it'd still be such an awful lot of money.' The housing shortage worried Ted even more than it did Kathie. When Ted's workmate asked him if he planned to marry Kathie, Ted replied: 'I would if I could get somewhere to live. It's getting tougher instead of better.' But when Kathie asked him the same question, his frustration really boiled over:

> Where would we live? We couldn't stay with your people; there's not enough room. And we certainly couldn't live with mine! Look Kathie, you've got to be sensible about these things. I know a lot of couples just like us who decided to take the plunge. They found places all right! Stinking single rooms—and thankful to get them. Both of them out working so they could pay the rent and live. Living in joints where it's a crime to even think of having kids. Moving from one bed-and-breakfast joint to another. Sometimes separated for months on end.

The couple's solution was to buy a block of land and build a house themselves. Owner–builders were not only featured on the screen, but also in novels and short stories. In John O'Grady's bestselling novel about life in post-war Australia, *They're a Weird Mob* (1957), the main character and his wife, Nino and Kay Culotta, live in a tent on their block of land in the Sydney suburb of Punchbowl, while they build their house at the weekends.

The experiences of fictional couples like Ted and Kathie and Nino and Kay merely reflected those of countless real-life couples. For example, in 1949, Clyde Jones, a returned army serviceman, borrowed £1500 ($3000) from the Australian War Service Homes Commission to build a modest-sized, timber house in the outer Melbourne suburb of Templestowe. Clyde did all but the plumbing and the electrical work himself, while his wife, Edna, 'battled and bargained' for building materials that were often in short supply. During the three years that it took them to complete the house, the couple lived in a two-room shack on the building site.

Many post-war owner-builders constructed the garage first of all, so they had somewhere to live until their house was finished. Local governments set the minimum size for a live-in garage at around 20 feet by 12 feet, which was large enough for a bathroom, a bed-sitting room and a kitchenette. The lure of an affordable 'tailor-made' house was the incentive to live in cramped and uncomfortable conditions, often without basic services, such as sealed roads and sewerage.

The 'never-say-die' spirit of post-war owner-builders prompted some romantic comparisons with the pioneers of the past. A.E. Mander, for example, saw the survival of Australia's pioneering tradition 'in the thousands of young couples building their own homes . . . [as] one of the most heartening sights to be seen in Australia today!' Similar sentiments were echoed in the United States. J. Paul Taylor wrote:

> By circumstances, most of us Americans are descendants of a type that one time planned, saved and packed up to leave the familiar and take a trip into the unfamiliar, the strange and the insecure . . . and whether it's a rub-off from one generation onto the other or a matter of heredity, there's plenty of proof that the same kind of American is still in force today.

Even professionally built houses were often sold unfinished, so that home owners could economise and add their own personal touches. In the Australian short story, 'Too Young to Marry' (1954) by Lois Kleinhaver, a young couple, Bob and Nancy, announced their plans to marry and build a house. When Bob's father asked how they intended to achieve the latter, Bob explained:

> Well, Nancy's father is going to lend us about eight hundred [pounds ($1600)] and I can get an ex-serviceman's loan and we know a fellow who's a builder—he's a friend of ours. He's going to do the actual construction work, and we're going to finish the inside—you know, the painting and papering.

Modernism versus featurism

Following World War II, the demand for new houses was so great that building materials were in extremely short supply. A poem published in the *Australian Home Beautiful* (1947) summed up this predicament:

> Short of nails, short of wood,
> And short of glass as well—
> Short of materials;
> Say, brother, ain't it swell.
> Short of fixtures, short of pipe,
> Short also of brick—
> Even short of mortar
> To make the darned things stick.

Until supply could satisfy demand, Australian governments attempted to conserve building materials by limiting the sizes of new houses and making sure that building materials were used effectively and not frivolously. Under these conditions, it is not surprising that a 'watered-down' version of modernism, a style of architecture which espoused 'less is more', became fashionable. Compared with other styles of houses, modern ones tended to have fewer internal walls and decorative elements, which helped to conserve building materials. They also tended to have easy-to-construct, boxlike forms, which suited owner–builders.

In 1947, the Melbourne architect, Ross Stahle, designed a modern-style house in Frankston, Victoria, for a couple who wished to build it themselves. Prefabrication of the timber wall frames meant that within a month of the architect's plans being completed, the whole framework of the house was erected. The living room separated the bedrooms from the kitchen and the laundry to reduce circulation space. Most of the furniture was built-in to conserve timber. As an indication of the scarcity of some building materials, secondhand bricks were bought from a school which had burned down and a bag of granolithic sand was supplied by a monumental mason.

To the bitter disappointment of some architects, many people disliked how modern-style houses looked. In the United States, one large building contractor was forced to build traditional-style houses to save his business after taking the word of a leading architect who claimed that modern-style ones were what everyone wanted. In Australia, many do-it-yourselfers reacted by making miniature houses in the form of doghouses and letterboxes in almost anything but the modern style.

Take doghouses for example (I shall discuss letterboxes in Part II). A drawing by the brilliant Australian cartoonist, 'Wep' (William Edwin Pigdon), in the humorous book, *So, You Want to Buy a House* (1961) by Cyril Pearl, shows a do-it-yourselfer blissfully making an ornate Queen Anne-style doghouse, which is in complete contrast to his own, bland, modern-style house.

'Gone are the old-fashioned plain-looking kennels,' wrote the author of an article on doghouses in Australia in the *Australian Home Beautiful* (1957). 'In their place are elaborate, expensive affairs, built in both contemporary and Olde English styles.' He also referred to an American article which showed how to build a spiral doghouse, a Cape Cod cottage doghouse, a doghouse with curved glass windows and padded walls, and a doghouse with a sliding glass roof.

In *Australia's Home* (1952), Robin Boyd observed that the family dog seldom slept indoors, but in a doghouse, 'sometimes elaborately made in the image of the house'. Sadly, Boyd's almost affectionate view of this sort of thing had totally vanished less than a decade later. In *The Australian Ugliness*, he ridiculed people for decorating their homes with red flower pots, storks with scarlet legs, yellow concrete rabbits, and gnomes in bright green coats—to name but a few of the things which he considered ugly. He coined the term 'featurism' to describe this innocent form of self-expression, which he defined as 'the subordination of the essential whole and the accentuation of selected separate features'.

Most architects did not fully appreciate the important placemaking value of such homely trappings until after the publication of *Learning from Las Vegas* (1971), written by the leading architects from Philadelphia, Robert Venturi, Denise Scott Brown and Steven Izenour. They strongly argued that things like wagon wheels, letterboxes on erect chains, colonial lamps, and segments of split-rail fence were the suburb's equivalents of the significantly expressive hodge-podge of Las Vegas, Route One and Main Street.

All work and no play makes Jack a dull boy

World War II forced industry to become more productive through better organisation and increased automation. Efficiency experts reduced jobs into sequences of simple tasks, and engineers designed machines which required no special skills to operate. This enabled management to hire lower-skilled and lower-paid people and to spend less money training them.

One of the serious drawbacks for many workers was a significant reduction in job satisfaction. An assembly-line worker who, say, performed one of the two hundred operations required to produce a component for a machine assembled thousands of miles away, missed the face-to-face contact with his own accomplishments. In the film, *The Wild One* (1953), the leader of a gang of bikers, Johnny (played brilliantly by Marlon Brando), explained that the bikers' violent behaviour was due to their unfulfilling nine-to-five jobs: 'These guys are nameless, faceless fry-cooks and grease monkeys all week, working at dreary jobs they hate. They've got to break out and be somebody, they've got to belong to something. They do violent things because they've been held down so long.'

The automation of factories and offices not only created more unrewarding jobs, but also more leisure time. In Australia, the normal working week was reduced from forty-four hours to forty in 1948. What is more, people anticipated the introduction of a thirty-six-hour week 'fairly soon', and a thirty-hour week 'within a generation'. The same thing also happened in the United States. In *The Hidden Persuaders* (1957), the author and social commentator, Vance Packard, said that the average worker was spending one hundred and twenty-five days per year away from the workplace, which was unprecedented. He also predicted that 'by 1960 people would be averaging thirty-seven-hour weeks, and by 1980 nearer thirty'. But a shorter working week meant that the workers who felt like they were missing something now had more time in which to miss it.

Psychologists and sociologists believed that men with aimless, unfulfilling jobs could regain much of their pride-in-achievement and self-esteem by engaging in do-it-yourself activities in their spare time. One expert from Harvard University concluded:

> All creativeness gives men solid satisfaction. In creating we feel that our ego is rounded out, our self extended. Even an infant of two years will protest if you take his toy in order to show him how to run it; he wants to do it himself. What hollow lives we live when everything is done for us; we feel like invalids. To do it yourself is the result of craving after health, potency, completeness.

At the other end of the job spectrum, do-it-yourself activities could also help men in extremely demanding jobs to relax after a hard day's work. The editors of *Better Homes & Gardens Handyman's Book* (1951) claimed: 'Aside from saving money, working with your hands can keep you calm in a troubled world. With hammer and saw, you can forget your troubles entirely. Or you can resolve them much more readily than if you were sitting in a corner, stewing and fretting over them.'

Medical practitioners advised business executives who suffered from stress to take up a do-it-yourself hobby, such as carpentry or metalwork, to help them to relax. This happened to the lumber tycoon, Solomon P. Hirzhorn, a character in *Trustee from the Toolroom* (1960) by the Australian novelist, Nevil Shute. As one of Hirzhorn's business associates explained:

> Some years ago Mr Hirzhorn had a bad spell with his health, and his doctors told him he must get himself a hobby in his home. Well, he started a workshop—not a wood workshop like the rest of us, but a real engineering workshop with lathes, milling machines, shapers, a drill press, oxy-acetylene welding, and God knows what. He took me down and showed me. I never saw anything like it. That's where he spends most of his spare time now.

This also happened to the American filmmaker, Walt Disney. When the stress of running a large company became almost too much for him to bear, his doctor urged him to take up a do-it-yourself hobby. Since Disney had always loved trains, he began building a backyard railroad. When the film critic, Bosley Crowther, visited the Disney studio in 1949, he was dismayed to find Disney 'totally disinterested in movies and wholly, almost weirdly concerned with the building of a miniature railroad engine and a string of cars in the workshops

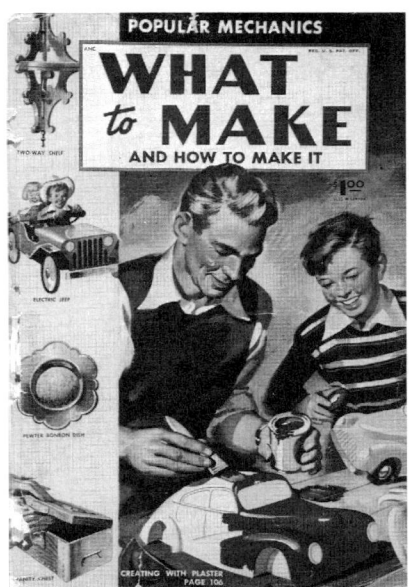 

A father and son work together in their home workshop on the cover of *Popular Mechanics What to Make and How to Make It*.

The cover of *Better Homes & Gardens Handyman's Book*. As the smug-looking muscle-bound handyman drills a hole in a piece of timber, his wife swoons with admiration in the background.

of the studio. All of his zest for invention, for creating fantasies, seemed to be going into this plaything,' Crowther said. But there was no need to worry, because Disney's backyard railroad lead to the development of one of his biggest and most ambitious ventures, Disneyland. 'The next thing you know, Walt was thinking about putting a railroad around here, at the studio,' said Ollie Johston, one of the Walt Disney Company's best animators. 'There was a guy in Los Gatos who had some engines that were used in the 1915 Pan American Fair in San Francisco, and Walt was thinking of buying those. Then he got to thinking there wasn't enough room here, and before long there was Disneyland.'

Hopeless handymen

Of course, not all do-it-yourselfers were skilled. Tom Rath, the central character in *The Man in the Gray Flannel Suit* (1955) by the American novelist, Sloan Wilson, grew to hate his little house on Greentree Avenue because, in all sorts of subtle ways, it 'proclaimed to passers-by and the neighbours that Thomas R. Rath and his family disliked "working around the place" and couldn't afford to pay someone else to do it'.

Perhaps not surprisingly, Sloan Wilson was a hopeless do-it-yourselfer himself. While he was writing *The Man in the Gray Flannel Suit*, he needed the assistance of his handyman–neighbour when the letter 'e' suddenly flew off his typewriter. According to Wilson:

> Staring out the window of the bedroom I used as a study, I saw that the lights in the house of my neighbour, Allen Tauber, were still on, and the sounds of a late party could be heard. Allen had a lot of tools in a cellar workshop, I knew, and he was expert at fixing things. Hurrying to his door, I interrupted a song fest with my unusual problem. Putting down his glass, Allen got a soldering iron from his workbench and his pretty wife, Jeannie, held a flashlight on my typewriter while he firmly attached the 'e' to it.

For many hopeless do-it-yourselfers, a lack of skill did not mean a lack of enthusiasm. When the Australian humorist, David Storrie, tried to make a picture frame, instead of making a square he produced 'something between a parallelogram and a triangle'. He went back and forth, cutting the picture to fit the frame then cutting the frame to fit the picture, until finally he ended up with 'a miniature frame which contained a picture of blue sky and nothing else'. To Storrie's great surprise, his wife never asked him to make anything else after that.

In 1952, the *Australian Home Beautiful* published a number of cartoons by the Australian cartoonist, John Frith, which depicted some of his own amusing misadventures in the home workshop. In one cartoon, Frith shortens the legs of a dinner table, but cuts too much off one leg. By the time he manages to get all of the legs the same size, the table is only a few inches high. In another cartoon, Frith's family risks life and limb to help him build a bookcase—even the family cat gets injured in the process.

It was almost 'cool' to be a hopeless do-it-yourselfer in the 1950s. They had their own how-to-do-it magazine, *Bitter Homes & Gardens*, and they were usually depicted as likeable characters. Take the American comedian, George Gobel, for example. In 'You Can Be a Handyman . . . Sure You Can!' (1953), Gobel claimed that his nagging wife, Alice, was 'a strong believer in this do-it-yourself business, except she doesn't believe in doing it herself; she believes in doing it myself'. Gobel also recounted the time he tried to fix a gooseneck lamp, nearly electrocuted himself, and finally had to seek help from a professional. He also innocently revealed that his near fatal accident was by no means unique: 'It was two days before the electrician could come out. He was real busy. That was a bad week for gooseneck lamps.'

It may have been alright to be a hopeless do-it-yourselfer in the 1950s, but sections of the community were unjustly categorised in this way. Gene Dreyfus, the vice-president of Cooperative Homebuilders in the United States, suggested to Vance Packard that Jewish men had neither the temperament nor the skill for do-it-yourself activities. Women were also unfairly classified as hopeless do-it-yourselfers. In 1956, the *Australian Home Beautiful* published a series of articles, 'Carpentry for Women', in response to an 'insistent demand in our reader-mail from housewives'. While the author of the articles, Alex Smith, claimed that 'the so-called weaker sex can be relied upon to turn out first rate carpentry', they were remarkably unchallenging, beginning with 'How to Drive a Nail', and ending with how to make a leg-rest. Smith's patronising attitude towards women was typical of the do-it-yourself industry in the 1950s. But during World War II, women had clearly demonstrated that they could do all sorts of tradition-ally male-oriented jobs just as well as—if not better than—men.

In fact, ironically, many women were compelled to learn do-it-yourself skills because their husbands and sons were hopeless handymen. As one unusually encouraging do-it-yourself expert told women: 'Don't keep asking for that extra shelf in the kitchen. Borrow his drill and screwdriver and do the job yourself. It's easy.'

The huge popularity of the 1990s TV show, 'Home Improvement', suggests that hopeless handymen are still around today. In this American sitcom, Tim 'The Tool Man' Taylor (played by comedian Tim Allen) is the likeable, all-thumbs host of a how-to-do-it television show, 'Tool Time'. Taylor seems competent, however, he gets into all kinds of trouble while attempting various do-it-yourself projects, both at home and on television.

Backyard inventors and madcap inventions

During the 1950s, tinkering in the backyard was not only a relaxing hobby, but also a profitable one—or at least this was what many do-it-yourselfers hoped. As Dickson Hartwell, the author of 'How To Get Rich in Your Own Basement' (1955), explained: 'The prospect of making a million dollars in your own garage or basement workshop has one advantage over discovering a pot of gold at the end of a rainbow. It's been done not once but hundreds of times.' He also claimed that 'your tinkering is most likely to pay off if you invent something new, novel, and useful for the home'. To prove his point, he described several backyard inventions, including windows that closed by themselves when it rained, an egg beater that could produce mayonnaise in a minute and a half, and a non-stick frying pan ('one of the newest home inventions'), which had either earned or promised to earn their inventors vast sums of money. Hartwell made achieving fame and fortune sound easy, but the chances of becoming the next Thomas Edison or Henry Ford were extremely remote, to say the least. Most of the do-it-yourselfers featured in *Profitable Hobbies*, an American magazine about people who made money from their hobbies during the 1950s, earned only pocket money from their efforts, if they were lucky.

In the United States, some do-it-yourselfers made crazy gadgets for fun. 'Professor' Russell E. Oakes of Wisconsin, for example, had made dozens of them, including a mechanical cigar lighter, a reader's armrest shaped like an open car window, and a mechanical doughnut dunker. During the 1950s, he made over one thousand public appearances, demonstrating his crazy gadgets to Boy Scouts, business associations and men's clubs. The American artist, H.C. Westermann, also created crazy gadgets, such as a 'Nouveau Rat Trap' (1965), a new kind of rat trap in the Art Nouveau style, and a 'Machine Dedicated to Spike Jones' (1976), a noise-making machine for the whacky bandmaster, Spike Jones. These witty contraptions also referred to the slavery of men to machines. Before he became an artist, Westermann was a handyman. After serving as a marine in World War II, he taught himself carpentry from how-to-do-it magazines and, while attending art school in Chicago, augmented his income by working as a handyman.

In Australia, do-it-yourselfers often made crazy letterboxes for fun. In 'Don't Be a Slave to Your Independence' (1955), a humorous look at the chaos sometimes wrought by do-it-yourselfers, Ken Collie wrote: 'The P.M.G. [Post Master General] has lost three postmen dragged giggling to the psycho ward through trying to figure out the cunning little letterboxes devised by some of our more inventive members.' Incidentally, Collie's observations also supports my theory that, in the Australian suburbs, novelty, do-it-yourself letterboxes are largely a post-war phenomenon.

Like hopeless do-it-yourselfers, backyard inventors were also frequently depicted as likeable anti-heroes, misfits and rebels, especially by filmmakers. In 'Malcolm' (1986), the Australian feature film about a simple yet ingenious backyard inventor named 'Malcolm' (played by Colin Friels), his letterbox is mounted on wheels so that it can travel on model train tracks from the front of his house to his bedroom window.

In the Disney feature film, *The Absent-Minded Professor* (1961), Professor Ned Brainard, a small-town backyard inventor (played by Fred MacMurray), accidently invents 'flubber', an anti-gravity substance which enables people and objects to fly, while tinkering in his home workshop-cum-laboratory. According to Richard Schickel, author of *The Disney Version* (1968), Brainard was loosely based on Disney himself. In 1954, *Time* described Disney as 'a genuine hand-hewn American original with the social adze-marks sticking out all over; he is a garage-type inventor with a wild guess in his eye and a hard pinch on his penny, a grassroots genius in the native tradition of Thomas A. Edison and Henry Ford'. It also quoted one of Disney's friends, who described him as 'a sort of visionary handyman, who has built a whole industry out of daydreams'.

Another backyard inventor is Wile E. Coyote, co-star of the cartoon series, 'Road Runner' (1948–66). In the course of trying to capture his main adversary, the lightning-fast Road Runner, the Coyote uses a host of unlikely do-it-yourself gadgets, such as a pair of jet-propelled roller skates, which

never ever work to plan. Chuck Jones, the animator who
created 'Road Runner', admitted he was similar to the Coyote.
In Jones's autobiography, *Chuck Amuck* (1989), he wrote:

> The Coyote is a history of my own frustration and war with all
> tools, multiplied only slightly. I can remember that my wife and
> daughter would start to weep bitterly and seek hiding places
> whenever they saw me head toward the tool drawer, if only to
> hang a picture. I have never reached into that devilish drawer
> without starting a chain of errors and disasters of various but
> inevitable proportions. Like any other man, I would rather
> succeed in what I can't do than do what I have successfully done
> before.

The economic and social circumstances that prevailed in the
United States and Australia after World War II fostered the
growth of a very popular do-it-yourself movement, which
encouraged men, in particular, to make everything from houses
to letterboxes. The ability to do these things—not always
successfully—was considered to be a measure of one's manhood. As a result, women were generally discouraged from
actively participating in do-it-yourself activities like carpentry,
although they were encouraged to play a supportive role. As
far as the history of Australian do-it-yourself letterboxes is
concerned, imagine the post-war do-it-yourself movement as
an iceberg and the letterboxes as the tip of the iceberg.

2   Home Workshop as Playhouse

The home workshop

During the 1950s, the home workshop was the centre of male-oriented do-it-yourself activities. In the 1974 Boyer lectures, 'Housing and Government', the Australian historian and social commentator, Hugh Stretton, listed a variety of things traditionally made in home workshops.

> Shelves and cupboards for the house; some good toys made for the children and a lot of crazy toys and constructions made by the children, often with secondhand bits of wood or metal or plastic that would otherwise go for rubbish; and dog kennels and rabbit hutches and cubby-houses from packing cases that would have gone for rubbish. Then go-carts for soap-box derbies; and when the teenagers start to earn, a sailing dinghy and trailer half-price because they were built from a do-it-yourself kit and some old car parts; a ping-pong table; an extension to the [home workshop] to shelter the trailer-boat and an extension to the verandah to shelter the ping-pong table; and some of the work of adding a sleepout when the kids each want a room of their own.

Let me add 'letterboxes' to Stretton's list of homemade artefacts.

The home workshop was commonly located in a garage or a shed in the backyard or—in the colder parts of North

A typical 1950s backyard shed.

America—a basement. Most do-it-yourself experts preferred a shed in the backyard, because dust and noise were kept well away from the house. Also there was no need to be overly fussy about the appearance of a shed, as it was usually out of public view. Everyone understood that the backyard was basically a service yard, characteristically 'casual, male, untidy, relaxed, spontaneous, and in its way, creative', according to the Australian landscape theorist, George Seddon.

Home workshops came in all shapes and sizes (as they still do) depending on a do-it-yourselfer's budget, the level of his interest, and the amount of space available in the first place. Mick's and Roy's home workshops in Melbourne illustrate this very well.

Mick is a retired metalworker who loves carpentry. In the 1950s, he migrated from Canada to Australia and brought his woodworking tools with him. After settling in Melbourne, he built a carefully designed and superbly outfitted workshop in his backyard, which has a place for everything and everything in its place. It faces south-east to capture the soft, even, natural light. The floor is polished timber boards and the walls are lined with plywood (salvaged from the boxes in which his tools were shipped to Australia), which helps to reduce dust. There are two beautifully made cabinets—one for hand tools and the other for power tools—which have specially designed drawers for nails and screws, power-tool accessories and technical drawings. More tools are arranged in an orderly fashion on wall panels. Various sized planks of timber are neatly stacked on shelves. Even the spaces above the ceiling and below the floor of the workshop have been specially designed as additional storage areas. Mick's home workshop is so neat and tidy that he and his wife, Barbara, often spend their evenings there together. He does his carpentry, while she does her knitting.

Roy is a retired engineer who happily spends most of his spare time maintaining the thirty-six rental properties in Melbourne which he and his wife, Carmen, own between them. Since so much of Roy's time is spent away from home, he tends to use his home workshop (formerly a washhouse) more like a storeroom than a work place. Although it looks messy, it is in fact very well organised. He keeps all sorts of possibly useful odds and ends in boxes, which he has very precisely labelled. For example, the label on one box reads: 'Rubber Bands, Elastic, Foam Strip, Spatula.' He keeps all of the tools he needs to do specific jobs in specially modified suitcases. Brushes, rollers, scrapers, and trays are stored in the 'painting' suitcase; nails and screws are stored in a suitcase fitted with compartments made from cardboard drink containers; buckets, cloths, detergents, and sponges are kept in the 'cleaning' suitcase; and so on. Thus, before he leaves home for work, all he has to do is pick up the correct suitcase for a particular job, confident that everything he needs is at hand.

Mick's and Roy's home workshops are like 'chalk and cheese' in many respects. For example, Mick's workshop is almost an extension of his living room, whereas Roy's is merely a glorified cupboard; Mick's tools are 'displayed' on wall panels, whereas Roy's are 'hidden' in old suitcases, and so on. I am not suggesting that one workshop is better than the other, but only pointing out that they are different.

During the 1950s, a home handyman was, ideally, 'king' of the home workshop and free to do whatever he liked there. Home workshops therefore revealed a great deal about some men's values and how they related to the world. Of course,

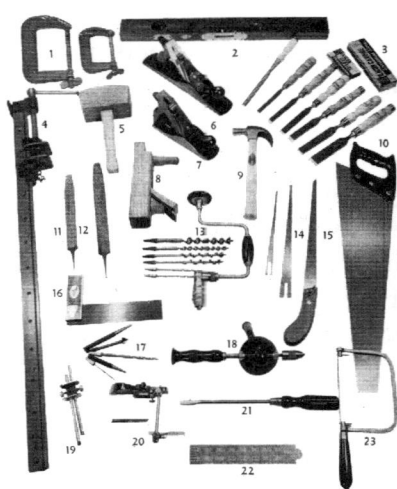 

During the 1950s, these twenty-three hand tools were considered to be essential for any serious do-it-yourselfer.

The cover of the October 1953 edition of *Popular Mechanics*: 'The workshop of a model home has caught Don's eye but Jane is determined he'll see the well-planned kitchen first'.

they were not unique in this respect, although they probably warranted more attention than they received. They may have been overlooked as mirrors of culture because they were so familiar, they were almost 'invisible'. Another reason may be that scholars considered them unworthy of serious study. To paraphrase the British architectural historian, Nikolaus Pevsner: 'A [home workshop] is a building; Lincoln Cathedral is a piece of architecture.' Certainly, as undervalued cultural icons, home workshops and do-it-yourself letterboxes have much in common.

Tools of the trade

During the 1950s, the home workshop was a huge 'toolbox', if nothing else. According to the Scottish essayist and historian, Thomas Carlyle: 'Man is a tool-using animal—without tools he is nothing, with tools he is all.' To tackle most household jobs, a do-it-yourselfer needed about forty different types of hand tools. The first ones to buy were the basic or 'primary' tools, including a brace and bits, chisels, a hammer, files, a mallet, a plane, pliers, a saw, and screwdrivers. Then came the acquisition of more specialised or 'secondary' tools, usually bought one by one for particular jobs, such as tin snips, a soldering iron and a hacksaw.

Do-it-yourself experts always suggested buying top quality tools, because 'good tools, like good friends, wear well'. Indeed, tools were often passed down from father to son, so they could be in use for a long time. After acquiring a kit of top-quality tools, a do-it-yourselfer had to take good care of them, otherwise, as one expert warned: 'The handyman who does not know how to look after his tools wastes a lot of time and a lot more money.' Buying low-quality tools was considered to be 'a waste of money, time and patience'.

Experienced 'old timers' believed that do-it-yourselfers should 'be able to walk before they can run—to learn to use hand tools before they attempt work with the machines'. On the other hand, the makers of power tools claimed that their products could transform hopeless do-it-yourselfers into skillful craftsmen: a Black & Decker portable power drill 'makes every man a Mr Fix-It'; a Shopsmith power tool 'builds egos, turns hesitant amateurs into craftsmen [and] its powerful hum awakens latent skills and old fashioned pride-in-achievement'; 'it's easy to be an expert with the K.B.C. Power Chief'—and so on.

Nearly everyone assumed that 'a well-equipped power workshop is the ultimate desire of all home handymen and hobbyists'. Since power tools were fairly expensive, the question of which ones to buy was hotly debated. The author of *Planning Your Home Workshop* (1949) claimed that the circular saw, the drill press, the bandsaw, the jointer, the jigsaw and the wood lathe were power tool's 'big six'. A multi-purpose tool, on the other hand, combined four or five power tools in one unit. Compared with buying each tool separately, a multi-purpose tool was usually cheaper and, perhaps more importantly, occupied far less space in the home workshop. In fact, 'multi-purposery' became a huge 1950s fad. One popular brand of multi-purpose tool even had its own cult following. The one hundred-member strong Shopsmith Club of Australia was formed in 1955, 'to promote the art of woodwork by study, provide practical demonstrations and foster the exchange of ideas'.

Due to the popularity of do-it-yourself activities, the demand for carpentry tools increased dramatically after World War II. This was reflected by the rapid expansion of Black & Decker, one of the world's leading manufacturers of power tools. Before the war, Black & Decker made power tools almost exclusively for professional tradesmen. But after the war, it also began manufacturing portable power tools for do-it-yourselfers. These tools proved to be so popular that, in 1951, Black & Decker opened a new factory in Maryland in the United States. One hundred and ten thousand square feet in area, this factory was more than doubled in size in 1953, and more than doubled in size again in 1956. In Australia, Black & Decker also expanded after the war, opening a new factory in Victoria in 1957.

Do-it-yourselfers devised some imaginative ways of cutting the cost of expensive tools. Whenever one of the amateur woodworkers who belonged to the Thursday Night Club upgraded his tools, he offered to sell the old ones to the other members of the club, thus allowing them to acquire quality secondhand tools at affordable prices. Many do-it-yourselfers also made their own power tools. In 1946, the *Australian Home Beautiful* published 'How to Build a Small Power Saw', and 'How to Make a Sanding Machine'. Even junk could be recycled to make power tools. The author of *Sixty Power Tools and How to Build Them* (1952) described how to make a power jigsaw from an old sewing machine. And one do-it-yourselfer from Melbourne made 'a gadget from pieces of wood and Ford valve springs, a few bolts and a couple of screws' which converted his buzzer into a 'quasi-thicknesser'.

During the 1950s, one alternative to either buying or making power tools was leasing them. Sherman Ashmore from Austin, Texas, rented out workshop space and equipment on both an hourly and a weekly basis, because 'many men who like to make things out of wood, can't or just don't spend the money on expensive tools that are needed for this hobby'. Some people thought that leasing expensive leisure equipment would be the way to go in future. In *The Hidden Persuaders* (1957), Vance Packard reported the views of one person who predicted that 'people would go to motels featuring their preferred kind of play: golf, gardening, power boating, *power tooling,* with the playthings being included as a part of the over-all charge' (italics added).

Tools were not only practical, but also beautiful. H.C. Westermann, for example, sometimes showed the people visiting his studio his tools of trade instead of his works of art. Certainly, tools can acquire a unique character through everyday use. Well-worn coal mining tools line the walls of 'Prospect V-II' (1982), a memorial to coal miners in Frostberg, Maryland, designed by the English-born, Minneapolis-based artist, Andrew Leicester. These tools are more than merely wall decorations, as they seem to uncannily retain the personalities of the coal miners who once used them. But the artist who is probably known best of all for making art with and about tools is the American, Jim Dine. One of his art works is discussed later.

Speed and sexuality

Most do-it-yourself jobs around the house were much easier to do with power tools, as the following 1950s advertisement suggests: 'What fun is there in sawing, sawing, sawing by hand? To those who first try an electric portable saw there is no going back to the old drudgery. It's easier, it's thrilling to speed through timber and it finishes the job almost as it [has] begun.' One do-it-yourself expert said the difference between power tools and hand tools was like that between driving and walking. Another claimed that the superior speed of power tools made it possible to 'get through the household jobs and still take in the Saturday football match or other outings. Machines can break your bondage to the home,' he said. Power tools were even supposed to make housework easier. Advertisements in how-to-do-it magazines showed women using a portable power drill to polish everything from furniture to their husbands' shoes!

During the 1950s, people were fascinated by speed. Naturally, this was exploited the most by the auto industry. In the United States, many cars of the period were equipped with a host of 'sporty', new, design features, such as wrap-around windscreens, chrome-plated speed-streaks, bomb-shaped fenders, beetle-browed headlights and aerodynamic tailfins. In *Fifties Style Then and Now* (1985), Richard Horn described cars like these as 'outrageous essays in pure style, visual odes to American ideals of power, mobility, and speed'. Even though Australian cars were not as flashy as American ones, the trend here was the same. The 1956 FE Holden sedan, for example, was longer, lower, heavier, and more powerful than its immediate predecessor, the 1953 FJ Holden sedan. The FE model also had 'a more modern, squarer appearance', and forty per cent more glass than the earlier FJ model.

In 'Vehicles of Desire' (1955), the British architect and critic, Reyner Banham, explained why 1950s cars had sex appeal:

> The top body stylists . . . aim to give their creations qualities of apparent speed, power, brutalism, luxury, snob-appeal, exoticism, and plain common-or-garden sex. The means at their disposal are symbolic iconographies, whose ultimate power lies in their firm grounding in popular taste and innate traditions of the product, while the actual symbols are drawn from science fiction, movies, earth-moving equipment, supersonic aircraft, racing cars, heraldry, and certain deep-seated mental dispositions about the great outdoors and the kinship between technology and sex.

Many social commentators agreed with Banham's views. Vance Packard, for example, wrote: 'After psychiatric probing, a Midwestern [advertising] agency concluded that a major appeal of buying a shiny new and more powerful car every couple of years is that it gives [the buyer] a renewed sense of power and reassures him of his own masculinity, an emotional need which his old car fails to deliver.' In *Sex, Drink and Fast Cars* (1986), Stephen Bayley claimed that the greatest marketing ploy of the twentieth-century was relating cars to sex. 'It is the car's power and its inherent conquest of natural limitations that lie at the root of its erotic appeal,' he said. However, sometimes the reason was more obvious. For example, one could argue that the vertical grille of the 1958 Edsel Ford looked like a vagina, while the sleek body of the 1961 E-type Jaguar resembled a penis.

In the closed world of the home workshop, power tools had much the same appeal as cars. They were fast and ultra-modern in design. A portable power drill, for example, was about ten times faster than a hand drill and, what is more, looked like Buck Rogers' ray gun. Power tools were also sexually suggestive—perhaps even more explicitly than cars. Since 'tool' was also slang for 'penis', 'power tool' suggested something extraordinary, to say the least. Therefore it is not surprising that power tools were extremely fashionable with men at the same time that, according to Vance Packard, 'men by the millions were yearning for evidence they were still indisputably and virulently masculine'. Packard believed this sense of insecurity had arisen because 'women had been invading so many [male] domains that [men] were being hard put to demonstrate that they were still he-men'.

During the 1950s, manufacturers of power tools perceived that their products could possibly provide men with the sexual reassurance they desperately needed. This may explain why men's portable power tools were usually much bolder in colour than women's household appliances, even though the two kinds of gadgets were very similar. The author of *How to Plan a Workshop* (n.d.) assured women that using portable power tools required 'no more mechanical ability than your usual household tasks in which you daily operate such electrical appliances as the vacuum cleaner, washer, mixmaster, etc.'. According to Robert Horn, the stylistic differences between portable power tools and household appliances 'is a clear instance of how, through something as seemingly neutral as product design, the rigid sexual distinction between males and females that prevailed throughout the 1950s was emphasized.'

The marketing of power tools was usually aggressively masculine. It was reported that Ward Bond, Rory Calhoun, Joseph Cotton, Glenn Ford, and George Montgomery (five of Hollywood's leading on-screen tough-guys) were all keen do-it-yourselfers in their spare time. Actors Alan Ladd and Ray Milland also appeared in magazine advertisements for portable power tools. As both of them were enthusiastic do-it-yourselfers, the advertisements took the form of testimonials. For example, the ad featuring Ray Milland claimed: 'Ray Milland's a handyman with tools—in his workshop, around the house, on his boat. So he knows what he's talking about when he suggests you put Home Utility Tools at the top of your shopping list for Dad's big day!' The message was loud and clear. Do-it-yourself activities were fit for 'real' men—or at least according to Hollywood and the do-it-yourself industry.

As far as speed, power tools and cars were concerned, it could be said that life eventually caught up with art. At the beginning of the twentieth-century, futurist artists and writers loved speed and machines as much as, if not more than, do-it-yourselfers did during the 1950s. In 1909, the Futurist poet, F.T. Marinetti, declared: 'We affirm that the world's magnificance has been enriched by a new beauty, the beauty of speed. A racing car whose hood is adorned with great pipes, like serpents of explosive breath—a roaring car that seems to ride on grapeshot is more beautiful than the "Victory of Samothrace".'

Kitchen versus workshop

The urgent need to increase industrial production to fight World War II helped to rekindle interest in the work of American efficency experts, like Frank and Lilian Gilbreth, who were among the first in the scientific management field and the very first in motion study. Frank Gilbreth was a 'larger than life' character, who practised what he preached.

> He buttoned his vest from the bottom up, instead of from the top down, because the bottom-to-top process took him only three seconds, while the top-to-bottom took seven. He even used two shaving-brushes to lather his face, because he found that by so doing he could cut seventeen seconds off his shaving time. For a while he tried shaving with two razors, but he finally gave that up. 'I can save forty-four seconds,' he grumbled, 'but I wasted two minutes this morning putting this bandage on my throat.'

Following the war, many of the labour-saving techniques that the Gilbreths and others had developed for the factory were also introduced into the domestic kitchen. Motion experts agreed that as a result of poorly designed kitchens, 'the average woman walks many needless miles in the course of a day'. In 'Your Kitchen: Friend Or Foe?' (1950), architect H. Dalton Clifford claimed that in the course of boiling an egg, a housewife travelled about one hundred and ninety feet in an old fashioned kitchen, but only about forty-nine feet in a modern one. The latter kind of kitchen was in fact a miniature factory designed to achieve a logical sequence of movement.

Efficiency was valued as highly in the home workshop as it was in the domestic kitchen. According to one do-it-yourself commentator, a typical, prewar, home workshop was often nothing more than a roughly built lean-to up against the backyard fence.

> Inside there might have been a bench and a few odd, badly used tools. But the place was generally a junking place for broken furniture, picture frames, paint cans, rolls of mildewed wallpaper, boxes containing boxes, empty blue bottles marked 'not to be taken', and sundry articles hanging from the rafters, unidentifiable because of the darkness.

After the war, however, the home workshop was considered by many people to be almost as important as the domestic kitchen. *Popular Science Monthly* (1956) featured a workshop that was 'as carefully planned as the mechanized kitchen'. One do-it-yourself expert claimed that 'architects have made [the home workshop] as important in their designs as the kitchen'. Another expert told do-it-yourselfers: 'You owe to yourself the feature of convenience in the [home workshop] just as your wife deserves convenience in the kitchen.' And yet another expert said: 'In these do-it-yourself days, a workbench is nearly as essential as the kitchen stove.' In other words, the home workshop was seen to be the male equivalent of the domestic kitchen.

How-to-do-it magazines published countless Gilbreth-like ideas suitable for both the home workshop and the domestic kitchen. In 'How to Put Your Tools Away' (1955), Edward Vaughn wrote: 'Arrange tools so that items you use together are spaced a shoulder's width apart—not right beside each other. That way, you can reach comfortably with both your hands for the tools, and put them away in the same manner.' In an earlier article on how to improve efficiency in the kitchen, 'Finger Tip Efficiency' (1951), Douglas Birk suggested doing something very similar: 'To save unnecessary trips from one side of the kitchen to the other, things that are used together should be stored together. To take an example, the saucepan, eggtimer and eggcups—required for the boiled eggs—should be stored together.'

Do-it-yourself experts suggested painting the interior of the home workshop in bright colours, not merely to gild the lily, but also to improve the efficiency of artificial lighting, to make cleaning easier and to discourage 'homesteading spiders and bugs'. Similarly, the colour scheme of the domestic kitchen was meant to improve efficiency. 'By a careful selection of bright, gay, livable colours it will be found that fatigue in the kitchen is reduced to a really astonishing degree,' wrote B.H. Brindley, author of *Australian Decorator and Painter* (n.d.). Once again, what was good for the goose was also good for the gander—and vice versa.

A place for everything

Since home workshops were often quite small, do-it-yourself experts encouraged handymen to utilise every inch of space,

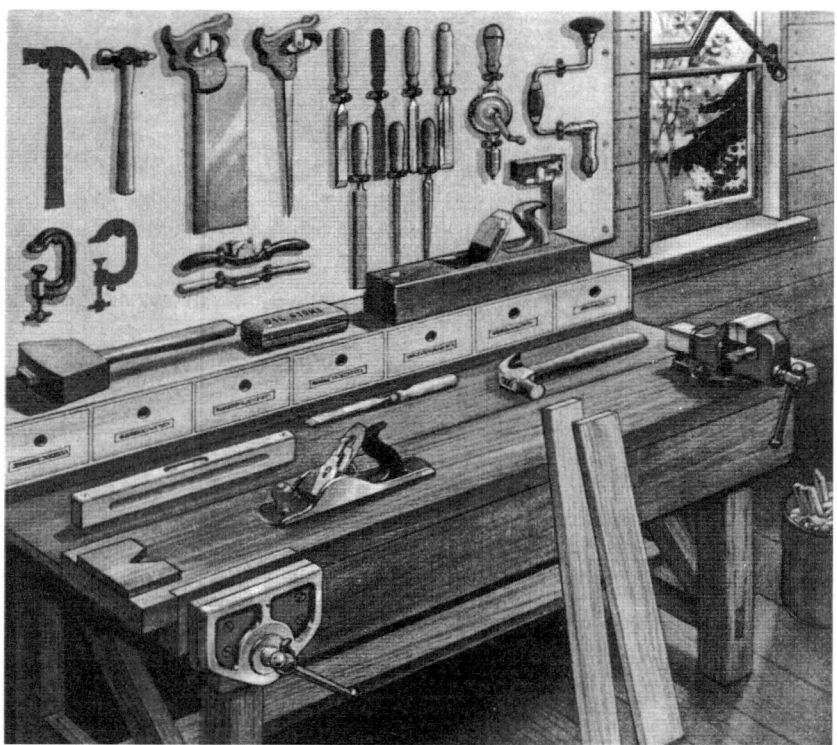

An orderly arrangement of tools. Note the silhouettes of the tools painted on the wall.

including the walls. Hand tools were often hung on the wall immediately above the workbench. This was very easily achieved when the wall was lined with pegboard, a perforated hardboard sheet introduced in the United States in 1953, and Australia in the following year. Tools were held in place with wooden pegs or metal hooks that fitted into the holes in the pegboard. Mounted on the wall in this manner, tools resembled exhibits in a gallery or a museum. However, if this was not efficient enough, the tools' outlines or silhouettes were often painted on the wall, to show at a glance where they were kept. As a result, the wall sometimes looked like a handyman's I.Q. test.

It was this kind of arrangement that inspired Jim Dine's assemblage-painting, 'Five Feet of Colourful Tools' (1962). Dine suspended some carpentry tools from a board attached to the top of a canvas, then sprayed them with coloured paints. This left silhouettes of the tools on the board and the canvas. He then rearranged the tools so they no longer corresponded with the silhouettes behind them. The American poet, Robert Creeley, said of this artwork:

> If, 'a place for everything and everything in its place' were ever to have a chance in this world, this painting would still come to haunt it. The act of hanging things up, putting things back, respecting things the way they were, is all wound in here in a way neither ironic nor pragmatic. Even who hung them up is very much a question.

In 'Mighty Proud, This Workshop' (1954), the American do-it-yourselfer, Charles Alft, wrote: 'A man's thinking can be cluttered up by cluttered surroundings. Why not make your workshop itself a project. Make it look as though you were proud of it—and then invite envious neighbour handymen for an "opening".' Those do-it-yourselfers who were obsessively proud of their home workshops usually put a lot of thought and effort into devising ingenious storage systems, such as keeping odds and ends in cheese boxes, cigar boxes, milk cartons and pickle jars; refilling empty toothpaste tubes with glue; putting a sheet of corrugated iron in the bottom of a drawer to hold files separately so they would not become blunt; and nailing a length of old garden hose to the wall to make a flexible tool rack.

An orderly home workshop was meant to be a means to an end, not an end in itself. However, as one do-it-yourself expert remarked: 'Some home workshops are so perfect you know the owner must do little but polish and rearrange his tools.' In *Man About the House* (1948), Norbert Engles described one such home workshop, which had a place for everything and everything in its place. Every power tool was tuned as finely as a musical instrument. The oil cups were always full, but never dripping. Even the nails were kept parallel in their compartments. But the only thing that had ever been made inside this immaculately kept workshop was a workbench.

The male sanctum

During World War II, people were often separated from their families and loved ones for long periods of time. This may explain why 'togetherness', the term made popular by the American magazine, *McCall's*, in 1954, was so important after the war. Family togetherness was about the whole family having fun together; watching television together; going for drives together; having barbecues together—and so on. The do-it-yourself industry was very keen to promote the fact that carpentry, especially, fostered togetherness between fathers and sons. On the other hand, do-it-yourself activities like this often segregated the sexes within the family, as the following 1951 advertisement for floor coverings pointed out: 'If your husband is like most men, he's probably happiest when he can spend some of his evenings and weekends working at a hobby. The only trouble is that when his interest involves special tools, he has to isolate himself down in the basement—and you find yourself a hobby widow.'

Many people believed this problem could be overcome by having a clean and tidy home workshop with lots of well-organised storage space and separate 'his' and 'her' areas, which was located near the family, not in the basement, the garage or the shed. For example, Mrs A.H. Shepherd from Launceston, Tasmania, 'objected to being a workshop widow'. The thought of spending the evenings alone while her husband worked at his pet hobby in a shed in the backyard did not appeal to her at all. So, when the Shepherds built a new house,

'Mr Shepherd included his workshop in the main plan. Instead of the usual cold and draughty shed (which is all most handymen have), it is a big, comfortable room, where Mrs. Shepherd can bring an armchair and [her] knitting.'

According to Steve Bedwell, author of *Suburban Icons* (1992), workshop widows still exist in the 1990s:

> Once in possession of a power tool . . . a man has the elusive excuse to lock himself in the shed. The excuse to close the rickety door on the rest of the world and settle back in the fold-up chair, put the races on the wireless and have a couple of coldies, usually in the presence of a mate brought in on the flimsy premise that he would be giving technical advice. Of course it's not all beer and horses in the shed; no, something has to actually be made to justify those Saturday afternoons spent in seclusion. I have it on good authority that the production of a lopsided bookcase or wobbly coffee table every four to six weeks is enough to maintain the facade.

Furthermore, Dr Michael Lee, a family therapist from Adelaide, South Australia, believes it is possible to divine the state of a couple's marriage according to their backyard shed or home workshop, which he classifies into three categories:

> Cramped, cobwebby, untidy? That [is] a Benign Shed, just somewhere you store the gardening things. Bigger, room for a fridge? Watch out, that [is] a Transitional Shed. Very big, containing a fridge, a bed, a computer, perhaps even a fax machine? Tragedy—you have a Malignant Shed on your hands, a place for a husband in almost permanent retreat both from conflict and from intimacy.

In post-war Australia, small houses and open-planning were cost-cutting measures which also happened to discourage privacy and encourage family togetherness, whether people wanted it or not. Under these circumstances, the home workshop was not such a bad place after all. In fact, it was often the only domestic 'sanctum' to which a man could retire after work. Thus, it provided a convenient and socially acceptable opportunity for married couples to get away from each other for short periods of time. As Dr Ernest Dichter, a leading advertising consultant in the United States, said: 'A man concentrating on his tools or his machinery is in a closed world.

He is free from the strains of interpersonal relationships. He is engaged in a peaceful dialogue with himself.'

Of course, the social segregation of men and women is not unique to Western culture. The Wogeo of New Guinea, for example, construct a type of building called a 'clubhouse', which is used exclusively by men as a dormitory, a class room, a meeting place, and a storehouse for sacred objects. Similarly, the Akwe-Shavante of Brazil construct a 'bachelors' hut' to segregate young boys from females while they acquire the necessary knowledge for manhood. Some interesting parallels exist between a ceremonial men's hut and a post-war home workshop. Both were primarily, if not exclusively, male preserves. Both were places of learning, where knowledge and skills were passed-down from father to son. Both served as a storehouse for symbolic, if not sacred, objects (ceremonial regalia in the ceremonial men's hut, and tools in the workshop).

Home workshop as playhouse

For Christmas of 1943, Diane and Sharon Disney, the daughters of Walt Disney, received a playhouse modelled on the Seven Dwarfs' cottage in the classic Disney film, *Snow White and the Seven Dwarfs* (1937). The playhouse was made at the Disney studio and then secretly reconstructed in the Disney's backyard on Christmas Eve. It had a white picket fence, its own little garden, gingerbread gables, a fully equipped kitchen with running water, and even a telephone. In 1945, *Look* published a photograph of Walt Disney in front of the playhouse and reported that he liked to tend its garden and cut its lawn. In other words, Diane and Sharon were not the only ones who enjoyed playing house, Walt did too. As the British architectural historian, John Summerson, pointed out in *Heavenly Mansions* (1949):

> None of us ever entirely outgrows the love of the doll's house or, usually in a vicarious form, the love of squatting under the table. Camping and sailing are two adult forms of play analogous to the 'my house' pretences of a child. In both, there is a fascination of the miniature shelter which excludes the elements by only a narrow margin and intensifies the sense of security in a hostile world. Less direct but even more common is the liking

Walt Disney stands in front of his daughters' playhouse which was modelled after the seven dwarfs' cottage in the Disney film, *Snow White*.

for models and houses in miniature. Many of us remember the enormous popularity of the Queen's Doll's House, shown for charitable purposes between the wars. The tiny cottage presented by the people of Wales to Princess Elizabeth exercised similar appeal. The concept of the diminutive in building exercises a most powerful fascination.

Some interesting parallels also exist between a playhouse and a post-war home workshop, especially one in the form of a backyard shed. Both structures were usually small and light-weight, sometimes even portable. The word 'cubby' is derived from 'cub' or 'kübje', archaic words meaning 'shed'. But more importantly, home workshops were often playhouses for men, small, cosy hideaways for daydreaming in as much as for working in.

A playhouse was frequently designed to be converted into a home workshop once the children had outgrown it. The *Amateur Craftsman's Cyclopedia of Things to Make* (1940) explained how to build 'A Fairy-Tale Cottage to Ornament Your Garden', which 'may be put to practical uses either as a playhouse for children or as a tool house'. In 'Playhouse for the Children' (1947), Alex Smith wryly stated: 'This little [play] house must not, in any way, be confused with a tool shed.' In 1951, *Australian House & Garden* showed how to make 'a sturdy playhouse [that] will delight any child, and may later be converted into a work or tool house'. In 1956, this magazine also published plans for building a 'Playhouse Now . . . Workshop Later'. *Popular Mechanics Workshop Annual* (1961) described how to construct a 'Garden Tool Shed Combined With Play Fort'. In 1963, *Science and Mechanics* featured a playhouse that, 'long after the children have grown up, can still serve as a potting shed, workshop, general storage area—even as a guest house'—and so on.

Walt Disney's home workshop, constructed around 1950, was a scale model of his father's barn. It reminded him of growing up on his father's farm near Marceline, Missouri, and probably helped him to grasp the important connection between small buildings and memory, which he clearly understood. This is evident from his comments on the design of Main Street, U.S.A., his idealised re-creation of Marceline's main street at Disneyland:

> It's not apparent at a casual glance that this street is only a scale model. We had every brick and shingle and gas lamp made five-eighths true size. This costs more, but made the street a toy, and the imagination can play more freely with a toy. Besides, people like to think their world is somehow more grown up than Papa's was.

Judging by this, it certainly appears that Disney's little barn-cum-home workshop was the real prototype for Main Street, U.S.A.. It was also Disney's playhouse because it housed the control panel for his backyard railroad.

Fighting the Cold War from the backyard

During the 1950s, many people had mixed feelings about nuclear power. On one hand, they appreciated the potential benefits of what they believed was clean, efficient, limitless energy. On the other hand, they feared the end of the world

as a result of nuclear war. This conflict is illustrated by contemporary attitudes to fallout shelters.

In 1957, the Science Advisory Committee of the Office of Defence Mobilization in the United States recommended spending a staggering $25,000,000,000 on the construction of fallout shelters throughout the country. Despite the dire implications of this recommendation, many people innocently regarded a fallout shelter as nothing more than the newest, chic accessory for the home. For example, Walt Disney constructed a fallout shelter in his backyard, which was disguised as a tunnel for his backyard railroad.

Wayne C. Leckey, author of *Popular Mechanics How To Build Your Own Garage* (1953), suggested constructing a fallout shelter inside the home workshop, which was consistent with its role as a retreat. In 1956, the British artists and architects, Nigel Henderson, Eduardo Paolozzi and Alison and Peter Smithson, collaborated on the now famous art installation, 'Patio and Pavilion', which, ironically, represented a toolshed after a nuclear holocaust.

Scholars believe that many people unconsciously transformed their fear of nuclear war into threats from outer space. In *Ogf* (1965) by the Australian author and broadcastor, Keith Smith, a jellybean-shaped flying saucer lands in George Cockburn's backyard. To cover this up, he tells his nosy, next-door neighbour, Fred Gadley, that it is really 'a new kind of building. New idea. A—a do-it-yourself kit. We're—er—going to use it as a toolshed.' This impromptu explanation reveals a lot about the quirkiness of the do-it-yourself movement and home workshops.

During the 1950s, the home workshop was a very complex and important place, despite its relatively small size and modest appearance. It was a place to pursue a wide range of creative do-it-yourself activities, including making letterboxes. As such it was a male 'sanctum'—the male-equivalent of the kitchen, no less—which housed important symbols of identity. It was the means by which a romantic minded do-it-yourselfer could travel back to childhood, for example, and re-experience the cosiness of the playhouse. And in troubled times, ranging from family squabbles to the threat of nuclear war, the home workshop served as a safe retreat.

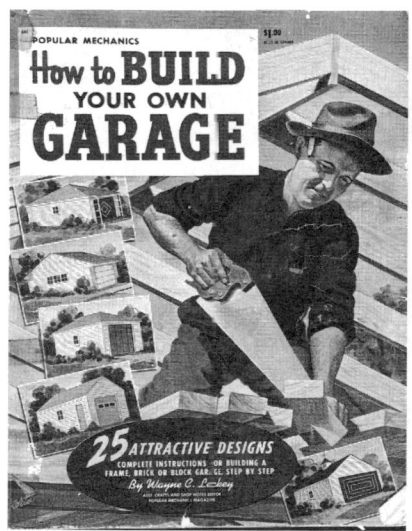 

The cover of *Popular Mechanics How to Build Your Own Garage*. During the 1950s, home workshops came in all shapes and sizes.

The cover of Keith Smith's humorous novel, *Ogf*. Ogf's spaceship was explained away as a do-it-yourself toolshed.

3   The Letterbox that Jerry Built

An Australian icon

In urban Australia, mail was automatically delivered to the front door until March 1909. The Australian Post Master General decreed that, there afterwards, if the front door was more than 100 feet from the footpath, a letterbox had to be provided on the front boundary of the property. As this distance has decreased over the years—currently, mail is delivered to the front door if it is within reach of the footpath—the number of residential letterboxes in use has increased. In 1996, Australia Post estimated there were over six million of these throughout Australia. Many are handmade and take unusual forms, such as cannons, ducks, fire hydrants, houses, petrol pumps, spaceships, teapots and washing machines. But despite the large quantity and eye-catching appearance of do-it-yourself letterboxes, they are often taken for granted because they are such an integral—almost 'invisible'—part of the Australian landscape. Nevertheless, they can reveal some interesting aspects of life and culture.

Do-it-yourself letterboxes are Australian icons in both the city and the bush. Since World War II, *Australasian Post*, a weekly magazine chiefly devoted to Australian popular culture, has periodically published brief items about unusual do-it-yourself letterboxes, ranging in form from a cheeky looking pig to the comic-book superhero, the Incredible Hulk. In 1968,

A slot for letters in a front door.

the *Australian Home Beautiful* conducted a nation-wide search for 'Australia's best letterbox'. Among those discovered was one like a cannon, another like the ferry, the Princess of Tasmania, two made from antique cash registers, and several like houses, including a Japanese-style house and a native tree house. In 1990, *Good Weekend* conducted a similar search and discovered letterboxes in the form of a bee, a bicycle, a farmer and his wife, the legendary Australian bushranger, Ned Kelly, and 'a toilet into which a mannequin has been shoved—two legs poke out and all correspondence is inserted in a familiar orifice'.

In the Australian suburbs, many do-it-yourself letterboxes reinforce the picturesque nature of their front-garden settings. Letterboxes which are made from tree trunks or resemble trees are obvious examples. Letterboxes like little houses appear to celebrate the traditional Australian dream of owning a detached house on a quarter-acre block of land in a leafy outer suburb. Letterboxes like castles, windmills and wishing-wells serve a decorative function similar to the much grander follies and ruins of eighteenth-century classical gardens. And suburban letterboxes made from obsolete farm equipment, such as old ploughs, tractor tyres and wagon wheels, help to reinforce

A teapot for a letterbox in Brunswick. People delight in recycling objects in unlikely ways such as this.

in an oblique way the fact that the front garden is a showplace and not a workplace.

Finding snails in the letterbox is a bizarre, yet common occurrence in the Australian suburbs. In *Dame Edna's Coffee Table Book* (1977), the doyen of suburbia, Dame Edna Everage (a character created by the Australian satirical performer and writer, Barry Humphries), lists among 'her' other books a little volume of verse, *Snails in the Letterbox* (1971). In an essay on Humphries, the Australian writer, television critic and broadcaster, Clive James, noted that another of Humphries' characters, Sandy Stone, had also referred to this peculiar phenomenon:

> Snails in the letterbox. It is a surrealist image which might have been cooked up by Dali in the presence of Buñuel, by André Breton in the presence of Eluard. But the words were said by Barry Humphries in the persona of the ruminating convalescent Sandy Stone, and in the Australian context they are not surreal. They are real. Every Australian, even if he lives in Sydney's Point Piper or Melbourne's Toorak, has at some time or other found snails in the letterbox. When you step outside on a dark and dewy night, the snails crunch under your slippered feet like

A tree stump for a letterbox in the Geelong suburb of Grovedale. But it could equally be some sort of arboreal shrine.

> liqueur chocolates. Snails in Australia are thick on the ground. Nothing could be less remarkable than a cluster of them in your letterbox.

Snails in the letterbox is the theme of the Australian children's book, *Snail Mail* (1986) by Hazel Edwards, which is based on the mail-nibbling snails that live in the author's own letterbox. In a letter, Edwards told me:

> One child wrote that *Snail Mail* was her favourite book. When I replied to her I enclosed her nibbled envelope to show that the snails had read it too. Her teacher wrote back, drawing a 'snail free zone' sign on the back. The snails did not nibble that letter. Either the Edwards' snails are literate or the letters were collected quickly that day!

Ironically, 'snail mail' is what enthusiasts of e-mail facetiously call ordinary mail because, by comparison, it takes such a long time to arrive at its destination.

Some types of do-it-yourself letterboxes are synonymous with the Australian bush, such as an open-ended oil drum or an old refrigerator or a packing case propped up on a couple of forked mulga branches', according to the author of *Mail*

An old stove was recycled as a letterbox outside of Broken Hill in New South Wales.
A refrigerator makes a very roomy letterbox near Mildura in Victoria.

for the Back of Beyond (1987), John Maddock. A letterbox made from a jerry-can fixed to the stump of a tree was used to represent the bush in an advertisement for the Victorian rural newspaper, the *Weekly Times*. And a letterbox made from an old refrigerator helps to establish a rural setting in Margret Wild's children's book, *The Very Best of Friends* (1989), a story about life on an Australian farm as seen through the eyes of William, the farmer's pet cat. Wild wrote: 'At the front gate there was an old fridge for a letterbox. Every morning William watched the postman put letters in the freezer, junk mail in the meat tray, telegrams in the butter box and parcels everywhere else.'

Bush letterboxes symbolise the isolation of the Australian outback. Clark Barrett, an American artist who now resides in Broken Hill, a remote inland town in New South Wales, enjoys painting bush letterboxes because they reveal 'a history of life in the outback'. One of Barrett's paintings shows three bullet-pocked, weather-beaten refrigerators-cum-letterboxes standing side by side on 'Dingo Trap Road'. Who would guess

'Three Fridges' by Clark Barrett.

that anybody lived in such an out-of-the way place, if it were not for these humble signs of life?

In *Children of Down-Under* (1962), a schoolboy named Don was shown collecting mail from a typical bush letterbox, somewhere in outback Australia. The text said: 'Don jumps on Bandi, his chestnut pony, and gallops down to the big letterbox by the road which leads past his father's sheep station. Sometimes Australian postmen are on their rounds for four weeks, because the inland regions are as big as several countries of Europe put together.'

Nowadays, mail is delivered to remote inland farms in a matter of hours by plane. Some 'flying posties' even take paying sightseers along with them to look at the bush and, more particularly, the unusual bush letterboxes. In 1990, I was a passenger on the mail plane that flew once a week between Broken Hill and Tibooburra in outback New South Wales. One memorable bush letterbox I saw consisted of a dilapidated refrigerator, minus the door, which contained a battered Esky (a portable icebox) for the mail, which was 'secured' with a log of wood. The use of recycled objects in this way also supports C.E.W. Bean's claim that 'it is still a quality of the Australian that he can make something out of nothing'.

Folk art at the front gate

In Australia, most people want to live in a house that is different from the others in the street, one that expresses their individuality. At the same time, most people do not want to appear odd or strange. Fortunately, an easy solution to this dilemma lies with the letterbox, which is the socially accepted vehicle for unfettered creativity and self-expression in the Australian built environment. It is widely understood that a crazy-looking letterbox in front of a house does not automatically mean that a crazy-minded person lives inside the house. As I explained earlier, both anecdotal and documentary evidence strongly suggests that, in the Australian suburbs, this is a post World War II phenomenon, chiefly due to the influence of the do-it-yourself movement. But why are letterboxes, in particular, singled out for artistic treatment?

One reason is that making a letterbox is a creative activity. Many letterboxes are made from junk or found objects. From an art perspective, they are assemblages (three-dimensional collages). In *Creating in Collage* (1967), Natalie d'Arbeloff and Jack Yates described four techniques for creating assemblages.

The first was: 'Allowing the shape and character of the found object to suggest an idea, then elaborating or interpreting that idea in a personal way.' Accordingly, a man from Ascot Vale, a suburb of Melbourne, made a letterbox like a dog from an old rabbit trap because the trap reminded him of a dog's jaws.

The second technique was: 'Putting found objects together and finding relationships between them.' This was how one letterbox in the Sydney suburb of Epping was designed. The letterbox and newspaper-holder were made from a cash register, the milk bottle rack was made from scraps of cast-iron lace, the top of the letterbox was decorated with some parts from a stove, and the base of the letterbox was made from a milk separator.

The third technique was: 'Giving new meanings to familiar objects.' Examples of letterboxes designed in this way include those made from petrol pumps, refrigerators, teapots and washing machines.

Finally, the fourth technique was: 'Beginning with a specific idea in mind, finding appropriate objects, then combining the idea with those objects.' This was used by a furniture removalist from the Melbourne suburb of Essendon, who made a letterbox from a toy furniture van. More about occupational letterboxes later.

It is interesting to note that the postal system is collage-producing by nature. The invention of the postage stamp, especially, set people all over the world gluing them on envelopes to make all kinds of patterns and pictures. One early fad was incorporating the postage stamp in an amusing drawing on the front of the envelope. In 'Humours of the Post Office' (1891), the author wrote: 'Often a gentleman is sitting on [a postage stamp] other times carrying it on his back, but the favourite place seems to be as the sign of an inn—"The Queen's Head."' But even without consciously trying to be creative, in the course of posting a letter the envelope automatically acquires writing, postage stamps, rubber stamps, stickers and other paraphernalia—it is, in effect, already a collage.

Many Australian do-it-yourself letterboxes are surrealist in character because they are made from found objects. The surrealist object is one that has undergone a dramatic change of role, so it no longer functions in the usual way. André Breton, the founder of surrealism, claimed that the only intellectual pleasure he had ever experienced was as a result of 'the spontaneous, extra-lucid and defiant relationship suddenly sensed between two things which common sense would never bring together'. Thus Breton would have probably appreciated Australian do-it-yourself letterboxes because many of them consist of familiar objects used in unusual ways, like the motorcycle helmet used as a letterbox. However, while do-it-yourselfers and surrealists both frequently incorporate found objects in their work, their primary motivation for doing so may be quite different. In the do-it-yourselfer's case, it is usually a matter of humour and making do with what is at hand for the sake of efficiency and expediency. Whereas in the surrealist's case, it is a deliberate attempt to shock the viewer and, in the process, extend the boundaries of art. But the effect on the observer is often much the same.

Australian do-it-yourself letterboxes are also consistent with the basic surrealist idea that ordinary, everyday things actually conceal something marvellous awaiting revelation. It may be as a result of looking at the world at large in this way that many of my thoughts about letterboxes appear to be echoed in Louis Aragon's surrealist novel, *Paris Peasant* (1971), especially in his descriptions of the Passage de l'Opéra. For example, Aragon said: 'Wherever the living pursue particularly ambiguous activities, the inanimate may sometimes assume the reflection of their most secret motives: and thus our cities are peopled with unrecognised sphinxes which will never stop the passing dreamer and ask him mortal questions unless he first projects his meditation, his absence of mind, towards them.' But instead of describing an arcade in Paris, Aragon could equally have been talking about the do-it-yourself letterboxes ('the inanimate') which reflect people's occupations, hobbies, fears, fantasies and aspirations (people's 'ambiguous activities . . . their most secret motives'). Furthermore, 'unrecognised sphinxes which will never stop the passing dreamer and ask him mortal questions unless he first projects his meditation, his absence of mind, towards them', could also describe the letterboxes that function as guardians of gates, but are taken for granted by the general public.

Another reason for the artistic treatment of letterboxes is their prominent locations. Australia Post recommends that, for the convenience of the postie and others, 'your mailbox should be clearly in view, and positioned on the boundary of your property, on the fence next to your driveway'. Coincidentally, this spot is very significant from a placemaking point of view. According to the American architectural theorist, Clare Cooper Marcus:

> Most people need to know where their domain ends and another begins. Researchers in the United States . . . Ireland . . . and England note that one of the first acts of a new house buyer is to define clearly the property lines—by planting vegetation or erecting a fence or low wall. Observations in British council housing estates where dwellings are now for sale indicate an

A letterbox disguised as a garden lamp in the Melbourne suburb of Mill Park. A stop light was recycled as a letterbox in the Melbourne suburb of Mount Waverley.

intense concern about boundaries and the symbols of ownership with a change of status from renter to owner.

Furthermore, Marcus states that, 'because of its symbolic meaning, the front entrance is more likely than any other part of the house to be personalised. Here especially one is likely to observe flowerpots, window boxes, ornaments, door mats, wind chimes, and so on. People like to see these personal touches as they come and go; they like visitors to see them also.'

A letterbox is an ideal vehicle for expressing one's individuality at the front entrance of one's home. This is usually achieved in subtle ways. B.H. Brindley suggested that 'a bright and attractively coloured letterbox will add much effect to the approaches to the house.' Some people carefully centre the number of the house on the front of the letterbox, while others plaster it higgledy-piggledy many times all over the letterbox. A few people have even made the number of the house the letterbox itself. Numbers are cut out of the front of the box to form openings for the mail. Usually '1' or '7' doubles as the mail slot, while '0', '6', '8' or '9' doubles as the newspaper-holder.

Most people would not bother to glorify their letterboxes in elaborate ways if the mail was not an important part of their lives. According to the author of *Waiting for the Mail* (1875), Mrs Nugent Wood: 'There are few people who cannot remember some time in their lives when the coming of the mail was to them blessedness or misery, poverty or wealth, hope or despair—nay, almost life or death itself!' People still anxiously await the mail, even though it is no longer the only reliable means of communicating over long distances, as it was in Mrs Wood's day. Thus, it is not surprising that some do-it-yourself letterboxes derive their symbolism from the mail itself and, what is more, reflect a longing for the mail. Many letterboxes resemble Australia Post pillar boxes—so much so, in fact, that some people have even been tricked into posting letters in them by mistake. One letterbox in the Melbourne suburb of Clayton South resembled an air-mail envelope. Painted on the letterbox were red, white and blue stripes, the words 'Air Mail', and a picture of an aeroplane. This letterbox belonged to a Greek family who liked to hear from their loved ones overseas.

While the mail may be an important part of people's lives, some letterboxes indicate that it is not always welcome. A prime example is the letterbox shaped like a tyrannosaurus in Parkville, an inner suburb of Melbourne. It has a spikey mane, small beady eyes, a gaping mouth where the postie puts the mail, a drooping black tongue, sharp white teeth and a sign that warns: 'Definitely No Junk Mail (or else).' Obviously, anyone determined enough to deliver junk mail to this house runs the risk of being bitten by the dinosaur.

A similar fate actually befalls the postie in Bev Aisbett's comic drawing, 'Postie' (1990). While pushing some letters through a mail slot, an ornamental brass lion comes alive and bites the postie on the hand. Likewise, in the American cartoon strip, 'Robotman', the letterbox which belonged to the horror-film character, Freddy Krueger, turns into a vicious dog and devours the postie. 'We have a problem with mail delivery on Elm Street,' said Krueger.

Far less threatening than these, but no less subtle, was the letterbox made from a toilet in the Queensland town of Anstead. A sign instructed the postie to put the bills in the

PART II

The Letterbox Phenomenon

This private letterbox in the Melbourne suburb of Clayton South was made to look like a public pillar box.
'Postie' by Bev Aisbett.

toilet bowl and flush the cistern. Similarly, a letterbox made from an old coffee grinder in the Melbourne suburb of Frankston has a notice directing the postie to put the bills in the grinder and turn the handle. Had letterboxes like these been around during the 1920s, then I am sure that Jack Gudgeon, the loveable anti-hero in Lennie Lower's brilliant, funny, Australian novel, *Here's Luck* (1930), would have had one. The following conversation is between Gudgeon and his exceedingly obliging postie:

> 'Only the one letter?' [asked Gudgeon.]
> 'There was one from the Gas Company, but I threw it down the drain like you told me to,' [the postie] answered huffily.
> 'That's right,' [Gudgeon] said. 'If you get one that looks as if it came from the Income Tax Department, put it down the same drain.'

Innovations, such as e-mail and faxes, may ultimately threaten the existence of letterboxes. The American pop artist, Dan Graham, anticipated something like this happening in his collage, 'Video Projection Outside Home' (1978), which shows a typical suburban house in the United States with a video screen out front instead of a letterbox. If the computer does replace the letterbox, then it may also become a vehicle for folk art. To some extent, this is already happening. Michaela Bjorksten, a textile designer from Melbourne, paints people's beige or grey computers in bright colours. And it seems that every man and his dog now has a home page, which is their personal statement to the world. Nevertheless, I suspect that letterboxes in their present form will not only continue to exist in Australia for a very long time, but also increase in number. In 1994 there were 152,561 more residential letterboxes than in 1993; in 1995 there were 139,033 more than in 1994; and in 1996 there were 191,187 more than in 1995, according to the annual reports of Australia Post.

It's a small world after all

'Ken's Joint' is written in large, decorative, wrought-iron letters on a letterbox in the Melbourne suburb of Reservoir ('rack off' is also written on the gate). This is one instance where a letterbox is a symbol of home. Several savings banks have also used letterboxes to represent home. An advertisement for the National Australia Bank asked: 'How do you get a home loan that's as individual as you and your home?' But instead of showing pictures of different people with their different houses, as one might expect, the advertisement showed pictures of different letterboxes. Two more home loan advertisements, one for the Commonwealth Bank and the other for the St George Bank, also featured letterboxes instead of houses.

On the other hand, the absence of a letterbox indicates no home. To prevent the delivery of mail to a vacant house in the Melbourne suburb of Northcote, the letterbox was covered with a white plastic bag. The 'lifeless' state of the house was dramatically reflected by the concealed letterbox, which almost resembled a corpse inside a body-bag. Thus it is not surprising that many people who do not officially require a letterbox, because their front door is within reach of the footpath, will still provide one or even 'fake' one for symbolic reasons. For example, the residents of one house without a letterbox in

Carlton, an inner suburb of Melbourne, painted the outline of a letterbox on the bottom of their front door.

In placemaking terms, installing your letterbox at the front gate is like staking out your territory. Traditionally, when a city was founded a stake was driven into the ground to symbolise the centre of the world. When Canberra, the capital of Australia, was founded in 1913, King O'Malley, the Minister for Home Affairs, drove a stake into the ground at the centre of the future city. Thus an anonymous patch of bush, chosen as the site of Canberra by a committee of bureaucrats and politicians, was sanctified as the symbolic centre of the world in Australia. By the same token, this special status can be revoked by simply removing the ceremonial stake from the ground. Thus 'pulling up stakes' is another expression for quitting one's home or job.

Do-it-yourself letterboxes may help to personalise the high-rise blocks of flats in several of the inner suburbs of Melbourne, which were designed by the Victorian Housing Commission during the 1950s and '60s for families on low incomes. According to the Australian architectural historian, J.M. Freeland: 'They were spartan buildings. Shorn of anything which could be considered, even vaguely, as superfluous, they

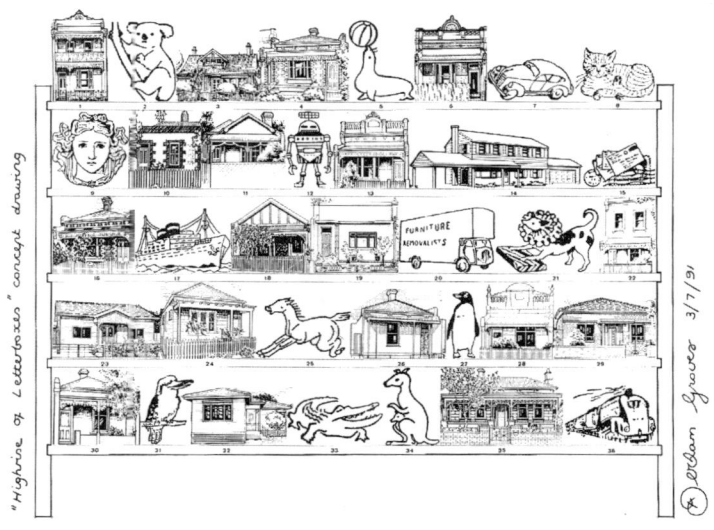

'Highrise of Letterboxes' by Derham Groves. A proposal to help to personalise the highrise housing developments of the 1950s and 1960s.

were barren, dull and graceless warrens arranged like children's blocks in flat, green swards of grass marked with signs which ordered bureaucratically "Keep Off".'

I believe one way to foster a more positive sense of place would be to encourage the residents of the flats to make their own letterboxes. This may lead to collections of unusual do-it-yourself letterboxes in front of these anonymous, filing-cabinetlike buildings, which would more accurately reflect the individuality of the residents. At present, the flats have banks of identical letterboxes which look like the niches in a cemetery wall where people's ashes are kept. This is hardly a positive symbol of home.

In *The Place of Houses* (1974), the American architects, Charles Moore, Gerald Allen and Donlyn Lyndon, stated:

> The relaxed recollection of house past or future or house eternal comes much more often in the images of 'little houses' that abound in the built world, in gabled porches, pedimented windows, in toy houses, and in the four-posted aediculas by which we set so much store. As architects we have enjoyed making such little houses inside as well as out, setting out for the inhabitants the same places for intensified habitation that were provided for saintly statues or the anointed in niches or on vaulted thrones in the ceremonial past, making places especially 'inside' which might allow some part of the mind to play house more freely than it might otherwise do, to add little house to house, to gild, we suppose, the lily, and embroider the claim of the inhabitants on a place that is special to them.

Once again, let me add 'letterboxes' to the architects' list of little houses.

According to the Canadian architect and author, Witold Rybczynski, the most beautiful house in the world is the one you build yourself. I agree with him. However, in the 1990s, very few people, wherever they live, possess the money, the skills or the time to build their own houses. In Australia, many people make letterboxes like little houses, which often have fine details, such as doors and windows, gutters and down-pipes, and TV aerials. This relatively simple do-it-yourself activity allows people to experience the self-satisfaction of building their own house, but on a small scale.

There are three main categories of letterboxes-cum-houses:

The do-it-yourself letterbox, 1955. Making a letterbox was sometimes a surrogate form of house-building.

generic houses; replicas of specific houses; and dream houses. The latter category is perhaps the most revealing. Robert, a single parent, and his three young children live in a rented fibro-cement house in 'Broadacres', a working-class suburb of Melbourne. He is quite concerned about living in 'this sort of house' and wants his children to have 'something they could be proud of when they approach the house'. So he built a large, fortresslike letterbox with things that he scavenged from a nearby rubbish tip, including brass plates, bricks, lumps of concrete, pieces of granite, terracotta tiles, timber mouldings and broken gadgets, such as a movement detector and a public address system. Robert is extremely proud of his letterbox, which obviously symbolises the kind of house he aspires to own.

Letterboxes like little houses are similar to architectural models not only in appearance, but also, more significantly, in helping people to feel like giants. In *Late-Twentieth-Century Skyscrapers* (1990), Piera Scuri discussed two portraits of famous American architects. One showed Cass Gilbert holding a model of the Woolworth Building, which he had designed, and the other showed Philip Johnson holding a model of the

Some letterboxes are miniature replicas of actual houses, such as this one in the Melbourne suburb of Preston.

AT&T Building, which he had designed. Scuri wrote: 'The architects' pose expresses possessiveness and dominion rather than affection. It reveals a desire to dominate, all the more urgent because it is unsatisfied—the desire to be the master (father) of one's own work. The model seems to satisfy a need that the finished architectural work—the skyscraper—denies.' Similarly, widely published photographs of Walt Disney show him looming godlike above various models of Disneyland.

Architectural models also help to reveal the 'big picture'. In Robert Venturi's proposed redesign of Copley Square in Boston, he included a miniature replica of Trinity Church, which abuts the square, as 'a means for explaining to a person the whole which he is in but cannot see all of'. Similarly, in Andrew Leicester's urban parks in Canyon City, Cincinnati and Los Angeles in the USA, he included miniature replicas of the local river systems, which, like the architectural models or plans in shopping centres, show people 'You are here'.

Letterbox crimes

In the Australian suburbs, the letterbox is usually located on the front boundary between the house (private space) and the street (public space), next to the driveway. Consequently, it is exposed to thieves, vandals and passing motorists.

A letterbox crammed with mail is usually a sign that no one is at home. To avoid presenting a thief with an invitation like this, the police recommend that letterboxes should be large enough to hold at least an entire day's mail. They also suggest that before people go away on holidays, they should cancel regular mail deliveries and arrange with a neighbour to collect any junk mail.

Since the letterbox is a symbol of home, an attack on the letterbox may be interpreted as an attack on the home, which explains why 'letterbox crimes' are often taken so seriously. One common crime is stealing mail from the letterbox. A letterbox in Fitzroy, an inner suburb of Melbourne, had the following messages written on it. To the postie: 'Please place mail under front door. Thank you.' And to the thief who was stealing the mail: 'Would the person who keeps removing our mail, please stop!'

Another common crime is stealing the letterbox itself. In 'Last Post for Young Hoodlums' (1991), Eileen Berry described how she had two letterboxes stolen and one set alight within the space of a few weeks. After something similar happened to a man from the Melbourne suburb of Glen Waverley, he conceived the bright idea of a portable letterbox. During the day he puts the letterbox in its customary position, but at night he keeps it in the garage, safe and sound under lock and key. Ironically, most people who have had a letterbox stolen do exactly the opposite. They firmly fix the new one in place. For example, a man from the Melbourne suburb of Preston had a letterbox made from an old, cast-iron, fire alarm. Pointing to its base, he told me: 'There's about four feet of concrete underneath there. While everyone else's letterbox in the street gets "knocked off", this one is as solid as a rock.'

In 1990, a gang of three young men blew up six letterboxes for fun in Glen Waverley, using copper tubes filled with gunpowder. In one newspaper report of the bombings, dramatically headlined, 'Letterbox Terror' (1990), the son of one of the victims said that bricks from his mother's letterbox were hurled across her front lawn, while pieces of the bomb itself had smashed through her kitchen window, dented a kettle, and landed in the lounge room. 'If mum had been in the kitchen at the time, she could have had her head taken off. There are certainly some crazies out there. There's just no reason for this,' he said. Before fireworks were banned to the general public in Victoria, incidents of this kind happened even more frequently than they do now.

Since letterboxes are usually located next to driveways, they are sometimes accidently hit by cars. But in the following case, a letterbox was deliberately hit by a car in order to carry out a vicious crime. In December 1990, Maurice and Bessie Watts, a retired couple from the Melbourne outer suburb of Doncaster, were sitting in their lounge room when a car slammed into their letterbox. Mr Watts went to assist the young, female driver, who was holding her face and muttering, 'I'm sorry, I'm sorry, I'm sorry.' After resting inside the Watts' house for a while, the woman was still too upset to drive to a nearby shopping centre, so Mr Watts drove her there in his car. When the woman returned later to collect 'her' car (it was actually a stolen car), she promised the Watts to pay for another letterbox, which Mr Watts estimated would cost sixty dollars. After the woman had left, Mrs Watts found a Christmas card from her, which read: 'Thanks for your kindness and assistance today. Have a nice Christmas and I'll make Santa's budget stretch to include a letterbox. Lisa Shaw.'

Ten days later, Shaw came back to compensate Mr and Mrs Watts for damaging their letterbox. Mr Watts recalled:

> When I opened the door, I noticed she was there with a chappie behind her with this box. I invited them in and then I said, 'Put the box on the table and sit down.' But instead of sitting down, the man walked toward the fireplace, turned around suddenly, and produced a gun from the box. He was swearing and cursing and saying, 'A hundred dollars for a letterbox, I'm going to kill you.' He just kept raving on saying, 'I'm going to kill you, I'm going to kill you'.

The man blinded Mr Watts by spraying mace into his eyes, tied him up, and threatened to shoot him if Mrs Watts did not reveal the whereabouts of the couple's money and jewellery. After the intruders had removed the Watts' valuables from their hiding place in the bathroom, they also tied up Mrs Watts, then fled.

Some letterboxes are symbolic guardians, such as this one in the Melbourne suburb of Essendon, which honours Leslie Charteris's private detective, Simon Templar ('The Saint').
A letterbox with a face in Frankston, Victoria.

Guardians of gates

The anecdotes mentioned above illustrate that fences and gates alone cannot always keep the outside world at a safe distance. This is why, traditionally, people have protected the vulnerable openings in boundary walls with magic. In China, for example, a house was protected from malign influences, including evil spirits, fires, sickness and thieves, by placing a 'spirit screen' in front of the door, magic charms above the door, and the portraits of fearless warriors on the door. Similarly, in England, a house was protected from witches by fixing a horseshoe above the door and burying iron objects underneath the threshold.

Few people would expect to find superstitious practices like these in contemporary Australia, but many people have turned their letterboxes into gate guardians. Letterboxes in the likeness of fierce-looking dogs, dinosaurs and crocodiles are prime examples. As it happens, the letterbox is situated in the right spot for a symbolic guardian. This may seem like an irrational thing to do, but as the architectural theorist, Juan Pablo Bonta, pointed out: 'Non-scientific beliefs about reality—the subject matter of the human sciences—exist in any society, even in those most sophisticated technologically.'

In the Melbourne suburb of Essendon, a man made a letterbox in the form of the haloed stick-figure used as a calling-card by Simon Templar or 'The Saint', the suave man-about-town created by the mystery writer, Leslie Charteris. The man chose this symbol for the letterbox because it deterred hardened criminals—or at least it did in Charteris's stories. But there was one problem. In Melbourne, a haloed stick-figure also symbolises the St Kilda Football Club. So the man painted the letterbox red and black, the colours of the Essendon Football Club, the team he actually supported, and also placed an Essendon Football Club bumper-sticker on the letterbox.

Many letterboxes take the form of the famous Australian bushranger and folk hero, Ned Kelly. He is an excellent guardian-cum-letterbox, because from a symbolic point of view he was notoriously fearless, and from a practical point of view the helmet he wore for protection strongly resembles a letterbox, since the eye slot resembles a mail slot. For some-what similar reasons, letterboxes also take the form of knights and soldiers. The head and torso of a knight in shining armour,

A knight in armour protects the mail delivered to a house in Preston.

originally an ornament for a bar or a den, was placed next to a letterbox in Preston. And two army helmets from World War I, one Australian and the other German, were hinged together to form a letterbox in the West Australian suburb of Floreat Park. Incidentally, the similarity between a helmet and a letterbox also inspired the creation of Flank Breeder, the neurotic character with a letterbox for a head in Bruce Currie's Australian, animated, short film, *Flank Breeder* (1982).

A letterbox built into one of the brick piers on either side of a driveway strongly resembles a turret, especially when the mail slot is vertical, like an embrasure, and the front fence is crenellated, like a castle wall. While this similarity may be 'accidental', several letterboxes are like castles. For example, in Babinda, a small country town in Queensland, one letterbox was expertly crafted in the form of Sleeping Beauty's castle, complete with turrets, towers, crenellations and a drawbridge. And in the Melbourne suburb of Mill Park, one letterbox is like a medieval keep or circular castle. For aesthetic reasons, front fences are banned in this suburb, so this letterbox-cum-castle is the only major boundary marker, which largely

A letterbox in the form of a castle in northern Queensland. As the saying goes, 'Every man's home is his castle'.
Letterboxes like churches in the Melbourne suburbs of Caulfield and Blackburn North.

accounts for its defensive symbolism, eye-catching light colour and huge size. Furthermore, given that a letterbox is a symbol of home, letterboxes like castles exemplify the old saying: 'Every man's home is his castle.'

Even more hostile than letterboxes resembling animals, rogues, soldiers and castles are letterboxes in the shape of weapons of war. In the Melbourne suburbs of Brunswick West and North Balwyn, two letterboxes are built to resemble cannons. In both cases, the guncarriage doubles as the letterbox and the barrel of the cannon doubles as the newspaper-holder. But technologically more up-to-date is the missile-launcher shaped letterbox in the Melbourne suburb of Ivanhoe.

Fortunately, for the sake of cordiality, letterboxes-cum-guardians are not always as aggressive as these examples suggest. Letterboxes in the form of little churches may invoke the peaceful protection of God. Some interesting parallels exist between these and vernacular household shrines in other countries. In the United States, for example, many Cuban–Americans put a shrine dedicated to a Christian saint in their front garden. This 'yard shrine' always faces the street and is usually located near the front boundary, so that the saint can protect the house. Similarly, in Thailand, many people put a little house for the guardian spirit of the land, Phra Bhum, in front of their own house. This 'spirit house' is usually located near the front boundary, so that Phra Bhum can frighten away potential intruders.

To some extent, all miniature buildings have magical powers. This point of view is shared by a number of observers of the built environment. In *The Most Beautiful House in the World* (1989), Witold Rybczynski said 'the architectural models that stand in office-building lobbies . . . have a talismanic, protective function. There is something magical about these little worlds.' And in 'Disneyland Down Under' (1978), an essay about fantasy gardens in Australia, Dennis Pryor asked:

> How do you frighten the little green men from outer space who might try to land on your own precious stone set in a silver-plated suburbia? You build an apotropaic structure, a tower with a propellor on it. You can scare off the devil with a model church at your front gate and you can fool the evil spirits by building a miniature house, swimming pool and resident dwarf.

Besides intruders, another serious threat to the home is fire. According to the Country Fire Authority of Victoria, 'most people have a cold inner dread of a house fire occurring . . . of waking to find our home engulfed in flames . . . of being burned alive . . . of losing loved ones'. Traditionally, people have relied upon talismans to protect their homes from fire. For example, in China, certain types of roof decorations, such as the dragonlike 'chi-wen' and a man riding a hen, were believed to protect buildings from fire. In England, the plant known as 'houseleek' was grown on roofs to protect the house from fire caused by lightning. And in Australia, do-it-yourself letterboxes made from inoperative fire extinguishers, fire hydrants and fire alarms appear to symbolically protect houses from fire. Interestingly, a 1991 community service announcement produced by the Country Fire Authority showed a woman frantically rounding up her young children as their house burned. Through the smokey haze she yelled: 'Quickly, outside! Wait by the letterbox!' And in a 1991 newspaper article on home safety, a Melbourne firefighter also recommended the letterbox as a meeting place for the family in the event of a fire.

A fire extinguisher makes a letterbox in the Melbourne suburb of Bulla.

Roadside architecture and do-it-yourself letterboxes

In *Learning from Las Vegas*, Robert Venturi, Denise Scott Brown and Steven Izenour encouraged designers to look seriously at the mundane and the tawdry as sources of inspiration. They developed a revolutionary style of architecture which was not based on traditional design paradigms, but on billboards, fast-food restaurants, nightclubs, shop signs, used-car yards, and so on. Likewise, do-it-yourself letterboxes could also be a source of inspiration for designers. Indeed, several interesting parallels exist between roadside architecture and letterboxes.

Roadside architecture sticks out like a sore thumb for sound commercial reasons. A clear relationship usually exists between the advertising 'gimmick' and the goods or services being sold. For example, the banana-shaped store in the New South Wales town of Coffs Harbour entices people to stop, look and—most importantly—buy a banana smoothy. In *What Do People Do All Day?* (1968), the children's author and illustrator, Richard Scarry, depicted a host of delightful shop signs, including a magnifying glass outside a detective agency, a pair of scissors outside a dressmaker's shop, a saw outside a hardware store, and a watch outside a jewellery store, which were inspired by the signs outside inns in Switzerland. And in 'Sculptural Advertising' (1927), the American architect,

An apple orchardist near Bendigo in Victoria has a letterbox like an apple.

Robert H. Orr, described with dismay the practice of placing statues of horses, cars, cows, bulls and bathing beauties along the roadsides in Southern California, to advertise theatres, petrol stations, dairies, restaurants and hotels.

Many people appear to have turned their letterboxes into roadside signs which symbolise their occupations. An apple orchardist has a letterbox in the shape of a big red apple. A bee-keeper's letterbox is in the form of a giant bee. A dairy farmer's letterbox is made from an old milk can. A grazier's letterbox is decorated with the plastic ram from a Golden Fleece petrol pump. A horse breeder has a letterbox in the form of a horse. An interstate coach driver made his letterbox from rocks which he collected on trips around Australia. A furniture removalist's letterbox is made from a toy furniture van. A truck driver fixed his letterbox to a roadside mile-post.

Some tradesmen make highly imaginative letterboxes using the same equipment, materials and skills they work with every day. An electrician's letterbox was made from heavy-duty, electrical cables, while the letterbox-stand was made from a heavy-duty insulator. A handyman's letterbox was formerly a toolbox. A motor mechanic turned a wrecked gearbox into a letterbox. A stone mason's letterbox was made from off-cuts of highly polished stone. And a signwriter's letterbox pro-

A motor mechanic from northern Queensland has a gearbox for a letterbox.

claimed, 'Merv Jennings Signwriter'. Letterboxes like the last two examples are more than metaphors for what people do for a living. They are also actual samples of their workmanship.

Do-it-yourself letterboxes can also symbolise people's hobbies, interests and loyalties. A household of 'bikers' from the Melbourne suburb of Box Hill North, painted 'Tattooed people do it better', and a picture of a tattooer's needle on their letterbox. A person who plays the drums from Corio, a suburb of Geelong, has a letterbox in the form of a drum kit. To celebrate the Collingwood Football Club winning the 1990 Australian Football League Premiership, one Collingwood supporter painted his letterbox in the club's colours, black and white stripes. Many new migrants to Australia have patriotically chosen letterboxes in the form of a koala in a gum tree. And a train enthusiast from the Melbourne suburb of Cheltenham made his letterbox look like a model steam locomotive. The boiler held newspapers, the driver's cabin letters and the coal truck milk bottles.

Of course, the bigger and brighter the letterbox, the easier it is to spot, especially from a car travelling by at sixty kilometres per hour. Take Doug Harris's do-it-yourself

A train enthusiast from Clayton North in Melbourne has a letterbox in the form of a steam engine.

letterbox, for example, which is a miniature replica of his house in the Northern Queensland town of Cairns. Harris said: 'If anybody asks me where I live, I just tell them to find the letterbox that looks like the house.'

Roadside architecture often reflects the 'genius loci'. For example, the orange-shaped store in Berri, South Australia, the statue of a giant lobster in Kingston, South Australia, and the pineapple-shaped store in Nambour, Queensland, clearly denote the produce for which each town is famous. Likewise, some do-it-yourself letterboxes and letterbox-stands also reflect the special character of their localities. The following examples reflect the fact that they are all located in waterside suburbs of Melbourne. In Mt Eliza, there is a letterbox-stand in the form of a seal. In Patterson Lakes, a letterbox-stand is like a ship's anchor, while around the corner a letterbox is topped with a clam shell. And in Palm Beach Drive in Carrum, there is a letterbox in the form of a miniature yacht.

Roadside architecture and do-it-yourself letterboxes can help to suspend reality by altering the normal spatial relationship between an object and an observer. An orange the size of a building makes the observer feel like a Lilliputian, while a house the size of a letterbox makes him or her feel like Gulliver. Even though roadside architecture is created for commercial gains and do-it-yourself letterboxes are created for self-satisfaction, the effect is often similar.

Australia does not have a long history of roadside architecture, unlike the United States, although we do have a recent history of do-it-yourself letterboxes, our own distinctive form of roadside folk art. Unfortunately, this fact has not been celebrated enough. In a letter, Robert Venturi said: 'I had no idea of this rich tradition in Australian popular culture.' I believe that designers in Australia could gain possibly as much inspiration from do-it-yourself letterboxes as their counterparts in the United States have done from, say, the Las Vegas strip.

An American icon

For how much longer will Australian letterboxes be the focus of folk art? In the past, Australia Post was quite happy for people to make their own letterboxes, even sponsoring an exhibition of do-it-yourself letterboxes in 1992, so long as they were accessible to the postie and at least 330 millimetres long, 230 millimetres wide and 160 millimetres high on the inside. However, in 1994, Standards Australia prescribed a set of rules for 'the design, construction and performance of mailboxes in both commercial and residential applications'. If these are ever strictly enforced, then it might be the end of this unique form of Australian folk art.

Would the standardisation of letterboxes in Australia inhibit personal creativity? The United States experience indicates that it might. Rural free delivery was introduced there on a trial basis in 1896. To receive this service, people living outside of metropolitan areas had to supply their own letterbox, which sometimes took an unusual form. In his annual report of 1899, the United States Postmaster General disapprovingly stated that 'tomato cans, cigar boxes, drainage pipes up-ended, soap boxes, and even sections of discarded stovepipe were used as mailboxes'. In 1906, the American painter of Wild West scenes, N.C. Wyeth, did several advertisements for the breakfast cereal, 'Cream of Wheat'. Wyeth's most popular ad, 'Where the Mail Goes Cream of Wheat Goes', showed a cowboy-cum-postie on horseback putting a letter into a letterbox made from a 'Cream of Wheat' crate. Clearly, the nature of these early American rural letterboxes was similar to that of many contemporary Australian letterboxes.

In 1902, the same year that rural free delivery became a regular service, the United States Post Office issued standards concerning the size, shape and accessibility of letterboxes. In 1915, the post office went one step further and commissioned one of its employees, Roy Joroleman, to design an officially approved letterbox. Joroleman designed a letterbox shaped like a quonset hut, which became known as the traditional rural mailbox. Originally, there were two sizes of these: one for letters (18½ inches long, 6½ inches wide and 7½ inches high), and a slightly bigger one for parcels (23½ inches by 11 inches by 14 inches). Nowadays there are three sizes: small (19 inches by 6½ inches by 8½ inches); medium (21 inches by 8 inches by 10½ inches); and large (23½ inches by 11½ inches by 13½ inches). Despite its name, however, traditional rural mailboxes may be found not only in the countryside, but also in towns and suburbs.

The traditional rural mailbox is recognised internationally as an American icon. While on vacation in the United States, several Australians have even purchased traditional rural mailboxes as souvenirs. One reason why they are so widely known is because they constantly appear in American cartoons and comics outside Bugs Bunny's burrow, Mickey Mouse's house and Woody Woodpecker's tree.

In the United States, at the turn of the century, letterboxes made from tomato cans and solid wooden 'Cream of Wheat' crates symbolised the old frontier, the Wild West. Likewise, during the 1950s, the ubiquitous traditional rural mailbox symbolised the new frontier, the sprawling outer suburbs. In *Here, of All Places* (1958), the British author and illustrator, Osbert Lancaster, remarked that 'in America it was not until the last cowboy was but a memory for the oldest inhabitants that the myth of the Frontier found widespread expression in architecture. For some years past, the higher income brackets have from time to time been accustomed to indulge their pioneer fantasies on dude ranches but it is only quite recently that the ranch-type home has become available in large quantities to romantic-minded commuters of Long Island and Connecticut.' Significantly, Lancaster drew one of these houses with a traditional rural mailbox out the front.

A cartoon by 'Claude' in the *New Yorker* (1952) suggested that a traditional rural mailbox was also a symbol of home. A man is horrified to discover that his visiting, out-of-town relatives have not only brought their suitcases, but also their letterbox. Obviously, they plan to turn his house into their home away from home.

According to Charles Moore: 'In real houses, however modest, details of craftsmanship and signs and artefacts are developed at critical places to tell us a story about the interior of the house, just as the expressions of the human face speak of inner feeling.' The letterbox is an excellent example of what Moore is talking about. In the United States, during the 1950s, a spic and span letterbox indicated a well-kept house. The need to keep up appearances provided schoolboys with an opportunity to earn some pocket money, painting people's letterboxes. In 1956, Edward Matre from Los Angeles, earned twenty cents for painting a small letterbox and thirty-five cents for painting a large one. Ted Hustead from Cottage Grove,

Oregon, not only painted the letterbox, but also stencilled the householder's name on it. He earned one dollar for painting a small letterbox and one dollar fifty cents for a large one. The schoolboys' enterprises were reported in *Profitable Hobbies*.

In the United States, a number of manufacturers make novelty letterboxes which look like aeroplanes, crocodiles, fish, football helmets, houses, lobsters, pigs, roosters and tractors. Ironically, some employ top designers to produce 'folk art' like this. The Markuse Corporation of Woburn, Massachusetts, for example, produces up-market, high-priced, novelty letterboxes designed by three leading American architects: Michael Graves, Stanley Tigerman and Robert Venturi. Graves' post-modern, villalike letterbox has a clerestory newspaper-holder. Tigerman's letterbox is a replica of his own, prize-winning, holiday house in Lakeside, Michigan. And Robert Venturi's letterbox is a little red house with a gable roof and a 'smoking' chimney, which represents 'an abstracted idea of a house, or in a more fundamental way, the element of shelter,' according to its creator.

In *Design for the Real World* (1974), the American designer and author, Victor Papanek, strongly criticised novelty letterboxes like these. He wrote:

> They are 'high-style' enough to be forced into obsolescence every few years and, incidentally, snow no longer slides off them. They will probably sell well in suburbia and exurbia and will take on some of the symbolic values of new status objects. The manufacturers are to be congratulated: many more mailboxes will be sold and, more importantly, many more can be pushed upon the public every few years as even fashion in mailboxes is manipulated.

Papanek's criticisms were mainly based on functional considerations. But one could argue that the symbolic and placemaking roles of letterboxes should carry equal weight as function.

With their creativity curbed by the introduction of the traditional rural mailbox, many people transferred their efforts to the supporting structure. According to the United States Post Office, a letterbox-stand can take any form except that of 'effigies or caricatures that would tend to disparage or ridicule any person.' In *Signs and Wonders* (1989), Roger Manley described some unusual do-it-yourself letterbox-stands in North Carolina. These included 'a very determined-looking carved and painted Uncle Sam . . . his beady stare appropriate for the home of an elderly man beseiged by tax men and Medicare functionaries'. A wooden man with a helmet and outstretched tree-branch arms, 'emblematic of the guardian role required at the potentially dangerous point of contact with the outside world'. And a 1500-pound, concrete angel designed to protect the mail. A number of American how-to-do-it books and magazines contained ideas for novelty letterbox-stands. *Popular Mechanics What to Make and How to Make it* (1948), for example, showed letterbox-stands in the form of an arbour, a covered bridge, a Spanish mission, tree stumps and a wagon wheel.

In 1992, I visited the country town of Marshall, Minnesota, in search of some unusual, do-it-yourself letterbox-stands. In the course of an afternoon's drive through the farmland around Marshall, I discovered two dozen examples, mostly made from junk, which took various forms, including a barn, a cowboy, a grain silo, a labyrinth of water pipes, a machine for husking corn, a running man, an oil rig, a tractor, Uncle Sam and a wagon wheel. Unfortunately, these distinctive symbols of the Great Plains of southwestern Minnesota may pass into history in the name of road safety. In 1995, the Minnesota Transport Department launched a four-year plan to remove heavy and inflexible letterbox-stands along highways, because people might drive off the road and hit them. If what has happened in the United States is any indication of what might happen in Australia, then the standardisation of letterboxes will force people to transfer their creativity to something else, which would be a great pity as far as colourful, front boundaries are concerned.

Clearly, Australian do-it-yourself letterboxes are much more than mere containers for the mail. Letterboxes are Australian icons. Nowhere else in the world do people express themselves through their letterboxes with quite as much fervour as we do in Australia. Letterboxes facilitate links with the outside world. Most people love to receive letters—or at least those that contain good news. Also people often pass the time of day with their neighbours while standing next to the letterbox. Letterboxes are symbols of home. What is more, they are sometimes also symbolic guardians of home. However, in the process of minding the mail and guarding the front gate, they are prone to hostile, guerrilla attacks. Letterboxes are vehicles for unfettered creativity and self-expression. They often imaginatively express, for example, people's beliefs, dreams, fears, occupations and sense of humour. The act of making a letterbox also allows people to participate in the building process at first hand.

4 Learning from Letterboxes

The letterbox exercise

Since 1990, I have been examining the subject of Australian do-it-yourself letterboxes with university students, primary school children and practicing architects and artists. One seminar I taught at RMIT, 'Decision by Design', looked at design in Australian society. It was intended for students outside of the design disciplines, which meant that their ideas about design were similar to the general public's. To illustrate the character of vernacular design, I talked about do-it-yourself letterboxes. I began by asking each student to design a letterbox on the spot. Even though they had no forewarning of this exercise and only a few minutes in which to complete it, they effortlessly designed letterboxes like birds, cats, dogs, fish and snakes; letterboxes in the form of houses and castles; letterboxes made from recycled computers, refrigerators and TV sets; letterboxes that separated official mail from junk mail; letterboxes in the form of clowns, Ned Kelly and 'skinheads'; and letterboxes that automatically conveyed the mail from the front boundary to the house.

In 1991, I set a class of ten- and eleven-year-olds from the Fitzroy North Primary School in Melbourne a similar exercise. However, I also asked them to construct the letterboxes they designed, using recycled cardboard boxes, plastic bottles and other odds and ends. Even though this added requirement may

have curbed the children's creativity, due to their limited
construction skills and also the limited range of building
materials available, they still made some highly imaginative
letterboxes, including a cricket bat, a football and a tennis
racket; dogs, monsters and a zoo complete with a newspaper-
holder in the form of a boa constrictor; castles, houses and a
Swiss chalet; an aeroplane, a helicopter and a space station
that supposedly launched a rocket filled with junk mail into
outer space.

Many of the letterboxes designed by the students from
RMIT and the Fitzroy Primary School were quite similar to
some actual do-it-yourself letterboxes. It is worth noting that
this was not due to my influence, because I did not talk to
the students about the iconography of do-it-yourself
letterboxes until after they had designed theirs. Of course,
some students may have been influenced by do-it-yourself
letterboxes they had seen. However, another explanation could
be that the placemaking concerns relating to the letterbox, such
as the vulnerability of the boundary between one's house and
the street, the need to clearly delineate one's territory, and the
desire to express one's individuality, produces an almost
'instinctive' set of responses.

Another seminar I taught at RMIT, 'Built Form and Culture', was about the 'anthropology' of building for
undergraduate architects whose ideas about design were probably more 'highbrow' than the general public's. Three lectures
and an assignment were on do-it-yourself letterboxes. Part One
of the assignment required each student to find ten do-it-yourself letterboxes and write about them. Part Two involved each
student designing and constructing a letterbox for a building
or a person of his or her choice. It is worth noting that Part
Two was done after Part One had been completed and I had
delivered my lectures. Due to the influence of these things and
also the students' architectural training, their letterboxes were
more self-conscious than normal. But when one takes a vernacular art form and attempts to re-evolve it, this is almost
bound to happen.

A prime example was Phillip Rowe's letterbox in the form
of a huge, golden penis for the Dandenong College of TAFE,
a trade school in the Melbourne outer suburb of Dandenong.
While it was undoubtedly meant to be amusing in the tradition

of Australian do-it-yourself letterboxes, it was far more than simply a crude joke. It reflected the college's penis-shaped plan, its location on *Stud* Road, and the fact that it had been constucted by a builder named *Dickey*. Rowe's letterbox also highlighted the contradiction in terms of the word 'mailbox', since 'mail' is homonymous with 'male' and 'box' is slang for 'vagina'. And finally, it was also reminiscent of the phallic stones or 'hermes' placed by the sides of roads in honour of the Greek god of boundaries, Hermes.

One of my favourite examples was John Scaramuzzino's letterbox for Antoine De Saint Exupery's literary character, the Little Prince. It was made from junk that Scaramuzzino had found around the house, including a bird cage, a chair, a wooden crate for bottles, a fruit box, a bedknob and a stool. Each of these items related in some way to a character or an incident in *The Little Prince* (1945). For example, the chair supposedly belonged to the Little Prince, and the wooden crate supposedly belonged to the Tippler, one of the Little Prince's friends. Furthermore, the overall appearance of the letterbox resembled the Little Prince's distinctive, star-studded overcoat.

About fifty letterboxes were produced by architecture students in 'Built Form and Culture'. Some of the others included:

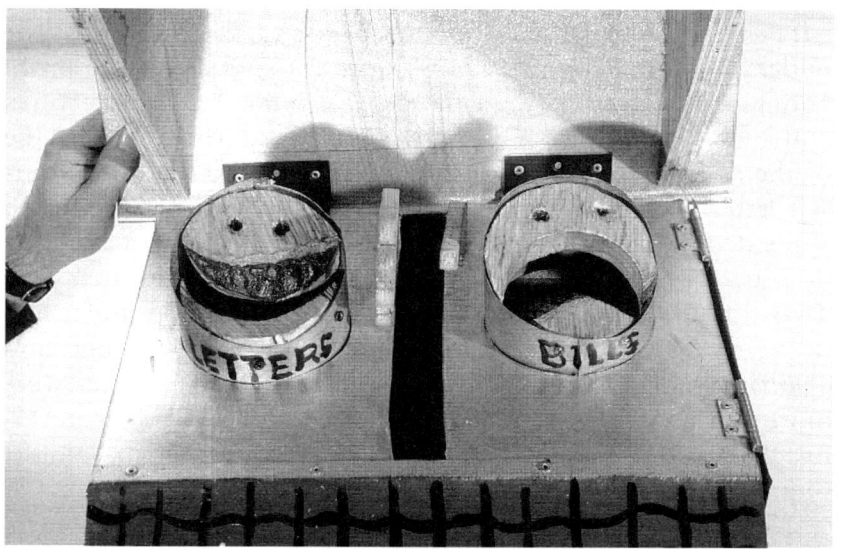

A letterbox designed by Warren Canham expresses happiness for letters and sadness for bills.

A letterbox in the form of a pair of binoculars for a house by the sea. A letterbox made from a stack of old books for a bibliophile. A letterbox like a flagpole and a sextant for Captain Cook's cottage in the Fitzroy Gardens in Melbourne. A letterbox like Luna Park for Luna Park in the Melbourne seaside suburb of St Kilda. A letterbox in a picture frame for a painter. And a letterbox in the form of an open mouth for a restaurant. Most importantly, this exercise enabled me to closely observe the creative process of translating an imaginative idea into an actual letterbox. In the 'real world' this usually happens in private, within the confines of the home workshop.

Letterboxes: An exhibition

In 1991, I recast the letterbox exercise as the subject of an exhibition entitled 'Letterboxes', by twelve professional architects and artists: Clark Barrett; Peter D. Cole; John Graham; Louise Lovett; Helmut Lueckenhausen; Maggie McCormick; Mary Newsome; Andrew Reed; Alex Selenitsch; Joy Smith; Akira Takizawa; and David Wong. Clark Barrett was from Broken Hill, but all of the others were from Melbourne. I invited these particular architects and artists to make a letterbox for a building of his or her choice, because this somehow related to things they had previously done. The tapestry artist, Joy Smith, for example, was interested in the Australian suburbs, thus her tapestries often featured decorative architectural elements, such as polychrome brickwork, wrought-iron lace and terracotta roof ornaments. The architect, Andrew Reed, had designed several doll's houses, which were similar in form and scale to many letterboxes. And the papier-mâché artist, Louise Lovett, was formerly a postie. However, most of the participants had not thought seriously about do-it-yourself letterboxes before, either as receptacles for the mail or as objets d'art. The woodworker, John Graham, summed up the group's previous attitude towards letterboxes:

> I suppose most of us hadn't thought of how important [letterboxes] are in one's life. For people waiting for word from overseas, even to just receiving junk mail on down days they have a large bearing on our lives. They can invite or repel, be angry or welcoming, they can be emotive, even an extension of

the ego. It's a form of pop art that can add a good deal of humour to our lives. We are fortunate that we are among the few countries able to do it and that Australia Post is reasonably flexible.

The painter, Clark Barrett, designed a letterbox for a farm about 100 miles north of Broken Hill. He adopted a surrealist theme because the name of the farm, 'Linray', reminded him of the surrealist artist, Man Ray. Thus the letterbox featured several surrealist icons: a miniature replica of Marcel Duchamp's sculpture 'Fountain' (1917), a urinal turned on its side and signed 'R. Mutt'; a covering of fur, reminiscent of Meret Oppenheim's sculpture, 'Breakfast in Fur' (1935), a fur-covered cup, saucer and spoon; and two f-holes, like those painted on the back of the nude model in Man Ray's widely published photograph, 'Le Violon d'Ingres' (1924). The letterbox also featured some symbols of the bush, including a miniature farm gate, sheets of rusty corrugated iron and the hand signal from an old truck. By mixing surrealist icons and folk symbols in this way, Barrett highlighted some similarities between surrealism and folk art.

The sculptor, Peter D. Cole, regarded the do-it-yourself letterbox as 'a conscious act of "making", the first point of contact with the space one has defined for him or herself'. Futhermore, he also believed that the letterbox was a significant boundary marker, since 'knowing the boundary or edge of that space is fundamental to one's existence'. Cole's letterbox symbolised the Australian landscape and the Southern sky. A long rod connected a full moon (the letterbox) to the constellation, the Southern Cross (the letterbox-signal and also, incidentally, the symbol for Australian air mail). This rod was fixed to the stump of a gum tree (the letterbox-stand) in such a way that the weight of the mail inside the moon caused the Southern Cross to change position from 'eleven o'clock' to 'twelve o'clock'.

John Graham designed a letterbox in the form of a pademelon, a small type of native Australian wallaby. Mail was dropped through the wallaby's pouch and removed by lifting the wallaby's tail. Graham also carried the Australian theme of his letterbox through to the letterbox-stand, which was a miniature replica of Uluru (formerly known as Ayer's

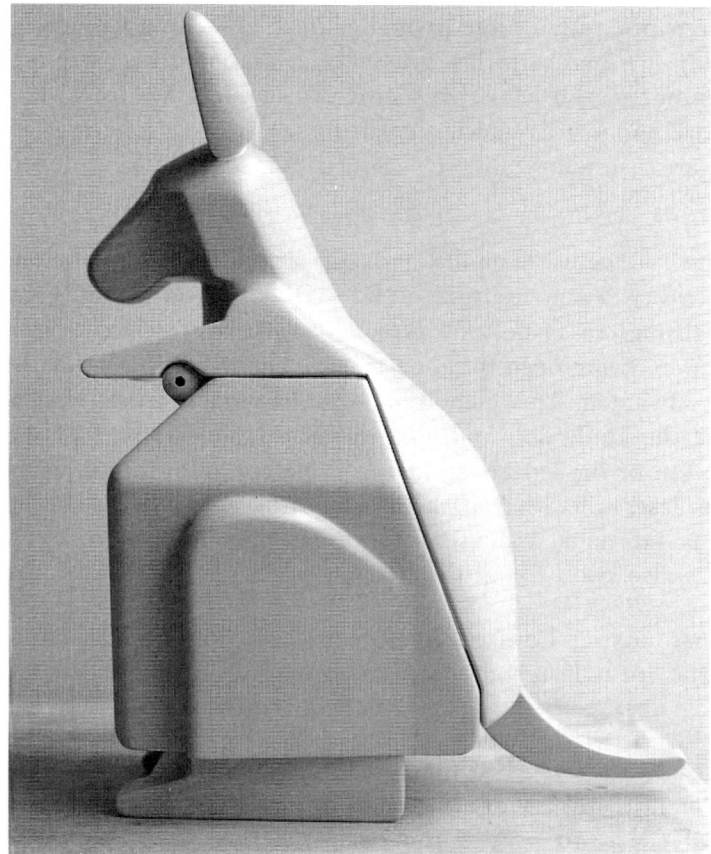

The pademelon letterbox designed by John Graham.

Rock). The letterbox was designed to be mass-produced from recycled plastic. However, the prototype was made of timber and sprayed with automotive paint to give it a manufactured appearance. Graham attempted to design a letterbox that was both functional and humorous, two qualities seldom found in professionally designed and commercially produced artefacts.

The letterbox designed by the sculptor, Helmut Lueckenhausen, took the form of a supernatural creature, standing on a pyramidal base. He described it as 'a gravestone for the living', because he saw similarities between letterboxes and gravestones as markers, guardians and symbols of self. Like many letterboxes, some Australian gravestones also symbolise people's occupations and hobbies, such as the airman's gravestone topped by a huge propeller in the Geelong Cemetery in Victoria; the blacksmith's gravestone shaped like an anvil and a hammer in the Marulen Cemetery in New South Wales; and the fireman's gravestone featuring a fireman's helmet in the Sandgate Cemetery in New South Wales. Lueckenhausen said:

> Marking . . . we use symbols, amongst other things, to stake-out our territory. From graffiti to 'DYMO' labels, we qualify by personalising. In respect of personal space, we welcome with reservation, being open to 'good magic', but warding off the evil or the unwanted. This dichotomy—the boundary 'fetish' that is at once the guide dog and also the guard dog—is part of the fascination of the letterbox. Just as cemetery architecture represents a last, somewhat pathetic cry of 'I have been', so the letterbox—through a mixture of pathos and hope—can say 'I am'. It's also good for getting letters.

As a former postie, Louise Lovett was well qualified to comment on the ideal letterbox. She said:

> It should be large enough to gobble up all of the junk mail delivered by the postie's competitors, and still have room for the bills, cheques and letters. It should also have a large slot with rounded edges, to protect the postie's cuticles, which can be damaged [while] putting mail into metal letterboxes with small, 'vicious' slots. However, the perfect letterbox from a postie's point of view isn't necessarily the most riveting one to look at.

When Lovett was a postie, a large, awkward, black dog used to follow her about, making a nuisance of itself by leaping over people's fences and squashing their flowers. When people started thinking that it was her dog, she complained to its owner. Two days later, the dog disappeared. Even though she had nothing to do with the dog's disappearance, she felt guilty every time she delivered mail to the dog's owner. So, 'to lift a postie's spirits, as well as help to ease [her] conscience', Lovett made a letterbox in the form of the black dog that went missing.

The ceramics artist, Maggie McCormick, made a letterbox in the form of a woman, which represented herself. McCormick was influenced by the architecture of Antoni Gaudi 'who created built shapes that reflected the shape of the people inside—a visual harmony'. She said:

> The letterbox, in its usual position at the gate, fence-line or property-line, plays the role of the guardian. I have extended this idea with this piece, which is a guardian of the thoughts only revealed through the visual form of symbols on paper—the letter. Collecting the post is always a moment of anticipation for me—the anticipation of thoughts revealed that may otherwise be left unsaid. Some of my best friends are letter-writers. I am a letter-writer. This letterbox brings these messages. The letterbox is usually associated with buildings and the people inside them. The relationship of the people to the building plays a role.

The printmaker, Mary Newsome, regarded the letterbox as 'an outward sign of life within the house'. Newsome's letterbox took the form of a Swiss roll and a lamington, which were the right shapes for holding rolled-up newspapers and flat rectangular envelopes. But unlike most things that are some-how transformed into letterboxes, these two popular types of cakes were much larger than life-size. Newsome's letterbox was a symbol of hospitality, like 'the door-knocker shaped like a hand holding an apple'. It was also a nostalgic reminder of postwar Australia, when women would compete among them-

The lamington and Swiss roll letterbox designed by Mary Newsome.

selves in the sphere of baking. According to Newsome, in those days, the culmination of a woman's art was to present a plate of perfect cakes on a hand-embroidered or crocheted doiley for afternoon tea. By referring back to the 1950s, Newsome was also trying to reclaim the days when people wrote long letters to each other.

Andrew Reed created a letterbox for a house that he particularly admired in the Melbourne suburb of Toorak, which was designed in the 1930s by the architect, Robert B. Hamilton. The main decorative features of the letterbox—the pilasters, the strapping, the roof pitched at forty-five degrees, and the colour scheme—were also the main decorative features of the house. But the special thing about Reed's letterbox was that it was large enough to accommodate the very bulky Saturday editions of both the *Age* and the *Weekend Australian* newspapers.

The letterbox designed by the architect, Alex Selenitsch, was modelled on a typical Australian cottage, which has three distinct parts: a verandah at the front, the main living area in the middle and a lean-to at the rear. Selenitsch bought a commercially produced letterbox, which was too small to hold large items of mail, and extended or 'renovated' it by putting 'a verandah of high-fashion numbers' on the front and a lean-to on the rear. He said 'houses that are too small are added to, and this letterbox is a shop-bought item that has been extended to comfortably take larger mail'.

Joy Smith's letterbox was based on the Federation-style, polychrome brickwork houses in the Melbourne suburb of Hawthorn. It was woven from unusual materials, including electrical wire and plastic bags, using a wire warp, so that it could be shaped into a three-dimensional object. Of course, tapestry is usually flexible and flat and woven with wool, silk or cotton. Smith's letterbox also highlighted the textile nature of both house-building and polychrome brickwork.

Trained as a temple carpenter in Japan, Akira Takizawa has lived in Australia since 1978. From two sections of bamboo, he made a simple, lightweight letterbox, which was in direct contrast to the letterbox-stand, a pair of upwardly reaching, intertwining arms and hands labouriously carved from the hard basalt stone found in the southeast of Australia, known locally as 'bluestone'. The hands were meant to lovingly

The Federation-style house-cum-letterbox designed by Joy Smith and woven from bits and pieces.

welcome the mail each day. They appeared to 'erupt' from out of the ground, just as the stone had done millions of years ago. Certainly, the everlasting nature of this volcanic rock was highly symbolic in Takizawa's eyes, representing not only relationships that endure over distance and time via the agency of letters, but also the legendary stoicism of posties: 'Neither snow nor rain nor heat nor gloom of night stays these couriers from the swift completion of their appointed rounds.' Takizawa named his letterbox, 'Nature Teaches Us the Importance of Living'.

The graphic designer, David Wong, made a post-modern shrine-cum-letterbox from found objects and recycled materials for a beach house. A beach house is a halfway-house for objects too good to be discarded at the dump, but not good enough or fashionable enough for continued use in the permanent home, like the dressing-table in Earl Derr Biggers' mystery, *The Black Camel* (1929): 'Charlie Chan . . . stepped to an old mahogany dressing-table, a handsome piece in its day, but now banished to the beach house.' A beach house is also sometimes a vehicle for unconventional architectural ideas, which may be a reflection of the atypical, non-routine, beach lifestyle. Wong said:

> Letterboxes hold more than pieces of paper. For those home alone or just peckish for news from 'the outside', the letterbox becomes the important symbol of communication and link to the world. The daily ritual of approaching this altar can become a religious experience. 'Dear God, just anything—even junk mail.' For these folk, the ultimate miracle would be the transformation of an empty letterbox into one stuffed and bursting with correspondence. And what would be more appropriate for this purpose than a converted roadside shrine, embellished with once-meaningful objects and mixtures of has-been styles not unlike the spirited decor and furnishings at beach houses. Clarice Cliff meets Fiji velvet painting; Robert Namatjira sits in a shell art frame. The inspired use of the expired can give a new lease on life to objects existing beyond their original use-by date. Likewise a letter can have the same effect on a human being. It is maybe this fear of obsolescence that locks the user and his/her letterbox in a fierce embrace.

Given the approach of the twenty-first century, I was surprised that not one of the artists and architects speculated on the future of letterboxes. Instead, they explored the same issues which concerned do-it-yourselfers. The letterbox as a symbol of place (Barrett, Cole, Graham and Wong). The letterbox as a symbol of self (Lueckenhausen and Newsome). The letterbox as a guardian of the gate (Lovett and McCormick). The letterbox as a little house (Reed, Selenitsch and Smith). And the need to communicate with others (Takizawa). However, by focusing on these familiar issues, the artists and architects—either consciously or unconsciously—emphasised the important role of the letterbox in its present form in Australian contemporary life.

The letterboxes created by the invited designers were displayed in major post offices in Melbourne, Geelong, Ballarat, Bendigo, Sale and Canberra. They were also displayed at the 1993 Royal Canberra Show in Canberra. The exhibition, 'Letterboxes', celebrated the letterbox as a unique form of Australian folk art, and also encouraged even more members of the general public to make their own letterboxes. One legacy of the exhibition was the 'Great Aussie Letterbox Competition', now a regular feature of the Royal Canberra Show. The inaugural winner of this competition, Laurence Cook, a sixteen-year-old student from Isabella Plains in the Australian Capital Territory, designed a letterbox in the form of 'the Aussie workman'.

Life in a letterbox

Since the late 1970s, I have been interested in 'mail art'. This relatively recent off-shoot of surrealism usually involves sending funny or serious items—not only letters, parcels and postcards, but also unpackaged objects like shoes and socks—via the official postal system. Such items may be exchanged between artists, sent to unsuspecting celebrities, circulated like chain letters, or exhibited in mail art exhibitions. However, the most important consideration is the process of creation, which includes not only the input of the artist, but also what happens to the mail art on its sometimes uncertain journey through the post, 'the writing, the franking and directing, the walk to the mailbox, the loyalty of the unknown henchman, the act of delivery, the opening, the perusal, the perceptions made and rejoiced at'.

Many artists create mail art using rubber stamps. These can be alphabet stamps, pictorial stamps of animals, people and objects, or stamps that convey preselected messages, such as 'Paid' and 'Urgent'. Since the rubber stamp is the unofficial symbol of bureaucracy, whenever people in any way appropriate, imitate, parody, or employ rubber stamps, they symbolically reclaim the validating tools of individual identity and hence participate in their own liberation.

Another popular way to create mail art is with unofficial postage stamps. The American artist, Donald Evans, was famous for 'inventing' countries and painting genuine-looking postage stamps to commemorate their culture, history and wildlife. Evans would put the stamps on letters, packages and postcards and post them to his friends. Since the postage was paid in the country of origin—albeit fictitious—the official post office would deliver Evans' mail art as usual.

The letterbox is to mail art what the gallery is to painting. To explore this idea, in 1993, the students in 'Built Form and Culture' designed letterboxes for some mail art created by the students in Judy Stone Nunneley's printmaking class at the Minneapolis College of Art and Design (MCAD) in the United States. Both groups discussed how, during the 1960s, mail artists had used the postal system to create accessible, spontaneous and irreverent art that was free of the art market, which also represented a new place for art in the culture, and a new way for art to serve as a tool of communication.

In general, the printmaking students' mail art tended to be serious, while the architecture students' letterboxes tended to be humorous. For example, the mail art created by printmaking student Rosemary Riskin featured ceramic figurines of women, printed images of women and pieces of coloured cloth all sewn together. Boldly printed on the back of this patchwork was 'Femail Art'. In response, architecture students Deborah Ross and Sam Stephens made an armless, semi-naked, overweight, female torso with a letterbox for a head. The letterbox was covered with adhesive vinyl used to line kitchen cupboards. A cup and saucer sat on top of the letterbox, and a cylindrical kitchen grater doubled as a newspaper-holder. Propped up against this suburban 'Venus de Milo' was a sandwich tray bearing the inscription: 'Bless this house. The women in this household slave until their arms drop off. No junk male!'

Printmaking student Ann Danielson's mail art consisted of an old and worn child's leather shoe in a timber box with a transparent lid. In response, architecture students Azian Huzairi and Julia Lam made a letterbox in the form of a giant shoebrush, complete with a tin of shoe polish. This was constructed in such a way that when the shoe mail art was put inside the shoebrush letterbox, a regular-sized shoebrush at the base of the letterbox-stand automatically shined the postie's shoes. Huzairi and Lam explained: 'The idea of trying to repair and restore the dilapidated shoe came to mind. Hence the concept of the shoebrush [letterbox]. However, we also wanted to do something for the postman, who brings us nice surprises through the mail. Hence the idea of the shoe-shine.'

The work of the students revealed some interesting parallels between do-it-yourself letterboxes and mail art. Both are frequently constructed using highly imaginative collage techniques, which often involve free association and paradigm shifts. Both collapse the boundaries between art and everyday life. Both often deal with serious issues in playful and humorous ways. And both gently subvert the official postal system, which could be seen to symbolise 'the establishment'. The printmaking students' mail art and the architecture students' letterboxes were jointly exhibited at the National Philatelic Centre in Melbourne in 1993, and at the MCAD Concourse Gallery in Minneapolis in 1994. This exhibition was called, 'Life in a Letterbox'.

In terms of Australian do-it-yourself letterboxes, the above seminars and exhibitions also illustrated the close relationship which sometimes exists between folk art and fine art. In 'But Today We Collect Ads' (1956), Alison and Peter Smithson described one facet of this relationship:

> Traditionally the fine arts depend on the popular arts for their vitality, and the popular arts depend on the fine arts for their respectability. It has been said that things hardly 'exist' before the fine artist has made use of them, they are simply part of the unclassified background material against which we pass our lives.

Conclusion

My interest in the postwar do-it-yourself movement, home workshops and do-it-yourself letterboxes developed as a result of looking at the Australian built environment through the eyes of a detective rather than an aesthete's. I believe that a detective, such as Sherlock Holmes, is a valuable role-model for anyone interested in discovering 'the extraordinary within the ordinary'.

Following World War II, the prevailing economic and social conditions in both the United States and Australia fostered the growth of an extremely popular do-it-yourself movement. It was another bond between Americans and Australians at a time when Australian popular culture was moving away from Britain and towards the United States. For many people on both sides of the Pacific, the do-it-yourself movement was one means of achieving an affordable, comfortable home. However, they were not merely motivated by utilitarian reasons, but also creative ones. Many do-it-yourselfers in fact created fantasy worlds. The ultimate example was Disneyland, which evolved from Walt Disney's do-it-yourself hobby, backyard railroading.

A common example was a letterbox mounted on a welded chain, which appeared to defy gravity.

The do-it-yourself movement provided a fascinating insight into sexuality and the demarcation of space in post-war Australia. Physically demanding do-it-yourself pastimes like carpentry were more popular among men than women. As a result, the focal point of these activities, the home workshop (where the letterbox was made), was regarded as the male equivalent of the kitchen. The portable power drill was also seen as the male equivalent of the mixmaster.

Currently, millions of people throughout Australia watch TV shows like 'Better Homes & Gardens', 'Burke's Backyard' and 'Healthy Wealthy & Wise', which showcase a wide range of do-it-yourself activities. Clearly, if the huge popularity of these shows is any guide, the do-it-yourself industry is thriving. And yet there seem to be fewer do-it-yourself letterboxes around today than there used to be. This reflects fairly recent changes in Australian society, including the decline in the importance of letters as a form of communication due to competition from faster, 'sexier' and increasingly more accessible alternatives, such as e-mail, faxes and mobile phones. While I am concerned about the future of do-it-yourself letterboxes, I hope that this unique form of Australian folk art will continue.

Australian do-it-yourself letterboxes are not merely receptacles for the mail. They are also Australian icons, symbols of home, symbols of self, and guardians of gates. The fact that many people—do-it-yourselfers—express these ideas spontaneously suggests they are important. However, even though do-it-yourself letterboxes often take unusual forms, such as animals, houses and recycled equipment and machinery, they seldom raise an eyebrow, because they are widely accepted as vehicles of unfettered creativity and self-expression in the Australian built environment.

Do-it-yourselfers offer whimsical insights into life and culture: our humour; our fears; and our dreams.

Select Bibliography

Alft, C. 'Mighty Proud, This Workshop'. *Better Homes & Gardens*, July 1954.

Alloway, L. 'The Arts and the Mass Media'. *Architectural Design*, February 1958.

Amateur Craftsman's Cyclopedia of Things to Make. Popular Science Publishing, New York, 1940.

Amory, V. 'How To Build a Work Bench'. *Australian House & Garden*, March 1956.

Aragon, L. (1971) (trans. Taylor, S.W.). *Paris Peasant.* Picador Classics, London, 1987.

Armant, N. 'Painting Mailboxes for Profit'. *Profitable Hobbies*, April 1956.

Asakawa, G. & Rucker, L. *The Toy Book.* Alfred A. Knopf, New York, 1992.

Australia Post Annual Report 1995–96. Australia Post Corporation, Melbourne, 1996.

Bachelard, G. (1958) (trans. Jolas, M.). *The Poetics of Space.* Beacon Press, Boston, 1994.

Banham, R. 'Vehicles of Desire' in Leffingwell, E. and Marta, K. (eds), *Modern Dreams: The Rise and Fall and Rise of Pop.* MIT Press, Cambridge, 1988.

Barkley, M.S. 'Hobbyists' Heaven'. *Profitable Hobbies*, July 1952.

Bayley, S. *Sex, Drink and Fast Cars.* Pantheon Books, New York, 1986.

Beal, R.G.W.J. *Jim Dine: Five Themes.* Abbeville Press, New York, 1984.

Bean, C.E.W. *On the Wool Track.* A. Rivers, London, 1910.

Bedwell, S. *Suburban Icons: A Celebration of the Everyday.* Australian Broadcasting Corporation, Sydney, 1992.

Bernard, E.M. 'Playhouse *Now* . . . Workshop Later' *Australian House & Garden*, May 1956.

Berry, E. 'Last Post for Young Hoodlums'. *Age*, 30 April 1991.

Berry, L.J. 'Two Talented Power Tools People!' *Australian Home Beautiful*, August 1959.

Better Homes & Gardens Handyman's Book (1951). Meredith Publishing Co., Des Moines, 1957.

Birk, D. 'Finger Tip Efficiency'. *Australian House & Garden*, December 1951.

Blainey, G. *The Tyranny of Distance*. Sun Books, Melbourne, 1966.

Blake, P. *The New Forces*. Royal Australian Institute of Architects, Melbourne, 1971.

Bonta, J.P. *Architecture and Its Interpretation: A Study of Expressive Systems in Architecture*. Lund Humphries Publishers Ltd., London, 1979.

Boyd, R. *Australia's Home*. Melbourne University Press, Melbourne, 1952.

——. *The Australian Ugliness*. F.W. Cheshire Pty. Ltd., Melbourne, 1960.

——. *The Walls Around Us: The Story of Australian Architecture*. F.W. Cheshire Pty. Ltd., Melbourne, 1962.

Brasch, R. *Permanent Addresses: Australians Down Under*. Fontana, Sydney, 1987.

Breitgraf, H.J. *Australian Country Mail Boxes*. Rigby Ltd., Sydney, 1972.

Brindle, B.H. *Australian Home Decorator and Painter*. Colorgravure Publications, Melbourne, n.d..

Bright, R. *Disneyland: Inside Story*. Harry N. Abrams Inc., New York, 1987.

Brotchie, A. *Surrealist Games*. Redstone Press, London, 1991.

Brown, S. (ed.). *Planning Your Home Workshop*. Popular Mechanics Co., Chicago, 1949.

Burns, K. et al. *Robin Boyd: The Architect As Critic*. Transition Publishing, Melbourne, 1989.

'Cars We Bought: 10 Years of Startling Changes'. *Popular Science*. February 1957.

Children of Down-Under. Hutchinson & Co. Ltd., London, 1962.

Christopher, J. & R. *Do-It-Yourself*. Pan Books Ltd., London, 1959.

'City, (The)' (1957) (video) in *Three In One: An Australian Trio*, Ronin Films, Canberra, n.d.

Clark, C.E. 'Shelter Magazines' in Taylor, L. (ed.), *Housing: Symbol, Structure, Site*. Cooper-Hewitt Museum/Rizzoli, New York, n.d..

Clifford, H.D. 'Your Kitchen: Friend or Foe'. *Australian House & Garden*, November 1950.

Collie, K. 'Don't Be a Slave to Your Independence'. *Australasian Post*, 31 March 1955.

Colomina, B. (ed.). *Sexuality & Space*. Princeton Architectural Press, New York, 1992.

Conroy, Paul. 'Robbed'. *Age*, 3 July 1991.

Curtis, J.R. 'Miami's Little Havana: Yard Shrines, Cult Religion and Landscape' in Browne, R.B. (ed.), *Rituals and Ceremonies In*

Popular Culture. Bowling Green University Popular Press, Bowling Green, 1980.

d'Arbeloff, N. & Yates, J. *Creating in Collage*. Watson-Guptill Publications, New York, 1967.

De Saint Exupery, A. (trans. Woods, K.). *The Little Prince*. William Heinemann Ltd., London, 1945.

Derr Biggers, E. (1929) *The Black Camel*. Mysterious Press, New York, 1987.

Derrida, J. (1980) (trans. Bass, A.). *The Postcard: From Socrates To Freud and Beyond*. University of Chicago Press, Chicago, 1987.

Disneyland: The First Thirty-Five Years. Walt Disney Co., n.p., 1989.

'Does It Bite?' *Australasian Post*, 9 May 1968.

'Do-It-Yourself'. *House & Garden*, May 1953.

'Do-It-Yourself: A New American Art'. *House & Garden*, June 1955.

'Domus'. 'How to Take Care of Your Tools'. *Australasian Post*, 6 September 1951.

Dormer, P. *Design Since 1945*. Thames & Hudson Ltd., London, 1993.

Doyle, Sir A.C. (1928) *The Complete Sherlock Holmes Short Stories*. John Murray, London, 1953.

Driscoll, W. 'It's the Day of "Do-It-Yourself"'. *Australian Home Beautiful*, August 1953.

Eager, A. *Dinkum Aussie Mail Boxes: Rural Art Treasures of Australia*. Child & Henry Publishing Pty. Ltd., Brookvale, 1986.

Edwards, H. (1986) *Snail Mail*. Collins Publishers Australia, Sydney, 1989.

Eisenhart, W. *The World of Donald Evans*. A Harlin Quist Book, New York, 1980.

Eliot, M. *Walt Disney: Hollywood's Dark Prince*. Birch Lane Press, New York, 1993.

Eliot, T.S. *The Complete Poems and Plays of T.S. Eliot*. Faber & Faber Ltd., London, 1969.

Engels, N. *Man About the House*. Prentice-Hall Inc., New York, 1949.

Epstein, R. *Mailbox, U.S.A., Stories of Mailbox Owners and Makers: A Celebration of Mailbox Art in America*. Gibbs Smith Publisher, Salt Lake City, 1996.

Farrugla, J.Y. *The Letterbox*. Centaur Press, London, 1969.

'Father Goose'. *Time*, 27 December 1954.

'15 Fast Jobs with Portable Power Tools'. *Better Homes & Gardens*, March 1955.

Fitzgerald, A. *Canberra and the New Parliament House*. Lansdowne Press, Sydney, 1983.

'Flank Breeder' (video). *A Currie Collection*. AFI Distribution Ltd., Sydney, n.d..

Frampton, K. (1980) *Modern Architecture: A Critical History*. Thames & Hudson Ltd., London, 1992.

Freeland, J.M. *Architecture in Australia: A History*. F.W. Cheshire Publishing Pty. Ltd., Melbourne, 1968.

Frith, J. 'Frith, the Down-To-Earth Home Carpenter'. *Australian Home Beautiful*, November 1952.

——. 'How To Make It'. *Australian Home Beautiful*, September 1952.

Gelber, S.M. 'Do-It-Yourself: Constructing, Repairing and Maintaining Domestic Masculinity'. *American Quarterly*, vol. 49, no. 1, March 1997.

Gilbreth, F.B. & Carey, E.G. (1949) *Cheaper By the Dozen*. William Heinemann Ltd., London, 1950.

Gobel, G. '*You* Can Be a Handyman . . . Sure You Can!' *Better Homes & Gardens*, April 1953.

Gorman, J.U. *How to Hold up the Mail*. Stephen Greene Press, Brattleboro, 1973.

Graves, P. 'Workshop in the Walls'. *Better Homes & Gardens*, May 1956.

Gross, F. (1952) *How to Work With Tools and Wood*. Pocket Books Inc., New York, 1955.

Groves, D. 'A–Z of Letterboxes, (The)'. *Qwerty*, no. 6, 1995.

——. 'Euphoric Coalface, (The)'. *Exedra*, vol. 6, no. 1, 1996.

——. (1991) *Feng-Shui and Western Building Ceremonies*. Graham Brash Pty. Ltd., Singapore, 1994.

——. 'Letterboxes'. Australia Post, Melbourne, 1992.

——. 'Walt Disney's Backyard'. *Exedra*, vol. 5, no. 1, 1994.

Haan, E.R. 'You'll Save with a Home Shop'. *Better Homes & Gardens*, November 1951.

Haddon, Dr A.C. 'Introduction' to Jayne, C.F. (1906). *String Figures and How to Make Them*. Dover Publications Inc., New York, 1962.

Halberstam, D. *The Fifties*. Fawcett Columbine, New York, 1994.

Hall, C.G. *The Mail Comes Through*. Macmillan Company, New York, 1938.

Hamilton, E. (ed.). *How to Plan a Home Workshop*. Delta Manufacturing Co., Milwaukee, n.d..

Hartwell, D. 'How to Get Rich in Your Own Basement'. *Better Homes & Gardens*, May 1950.

Haskell, B. *H.C. Westermann*. Whitney Museum of American Art, New York, 1978.

Heimann, J. & Georges, R. (1980). *California Crazy: Roadside Vernacular Architecture*. Chronicle Books, San Francisco, 1985.

Held, J. *Mail Art: An Annotated Bibliography*. Scarecrow Press, Metuchen, 1991.

'Here's a New Way to Organize Storage'. *Better Homes & Gardens*, September 1953.

'Hobby World, (This)'. *Profitable Hobbies*, May 1953.

'How to Help Your Postie Deliver Your Mail Early and Safely'. Australia Post, n.p., July 1990.

'How to Prevent and Survive House Fires'. Country Fire Authority, n.p., August 1988.

Hilton, P. 'That's a Good Idea!' *Australian Home Beautiful*, December 1958.

Historic Chinese Architecture. Qinghua University Press, Beijing, 1985.

Hitchings, B. 'Mailboxes Follow the Letter of the Law'. *New Home Magazine*, no. 39, 15–21 October 1994.

Hogan, J. 'Bungalow Built by Two'. *Australian Home Beautiful*, July 1954.

Holden Story, (The). General Motors–Holden's Corporate Relations Department, Melbourne, n.d..

Hollis, R. & Sibley, B. *The Disney Studio Story*. Crown Publishers Inc., New York, 1988.

'Home Improver?' *This Week*, 15 May 1994.

Horn, R. *Fifties Style Then and Now*. Columbus Books, Bromley, 1985.

Huff, D. 'Dripless Paint Looks Like Jelly, But Liquefies as You Brush It'. *Popular Science*, April 1956.

'Humours of the Post Office'. *Strand Magazine*, vol. 1, January–June 1891.

Humphries, B. *Dame Edna's Coffee Table Book: A Guide To Gracious Living and the Finer Things of Life By One of the First Ladies of World Theatre*. Australian Publishing Co. Pty. Ltd., Sydney, 1977.

'Is Your Number Showing?' *Australasian Handyman*, January 1948.

Izenour, S. 'Ducks and Decorated Sheds' in Maddex D. (ed.), *Built in the U.S.A.: American Buildings from Airports To Zoos*, Preservation Press, Washington D.C., 1985.

Jackson, J.B. *Discovering the Vernacular Landscape*. Yale University Press, New Haven, 1984.

——. *The Necessity for Ruins and Other Topics*. University of Massachusetts Press, Amherst, 1980.

——. *A Sense of Place, a Sense of Time*. Yale University Press, New Haven, 1994.

James, C. (1988) *Snakecharmers in Texas*. Pan Books Ltd., London, 1989.

Jordon, D.K. (1972) *Gods, Ghosts and Ancestors: Folk Religion in a Taiwanese Village*. Caves Books Ltd., Taipei, 1989.

Jones, C. *Chuck Amuck*. Avon Books, New York, 1989.

Judy, W.M. 'Details Make a Workshop Good'. *Better Homes & Gardens*, November 1954.

Kleinhaver, L. 'Too Young to Marry'. *Australian Women's Weekly*, 24 February 1954.

Klippel, N. '101 Ideas for One Panel of Pegboard'. *Australian Homemaker*, October 1956.

Lancaster, O. *Here, of All Places*. Houghton Mifflin Co., Boston, 1958.

Lantz, W. *Woody Woodpecker's Peck of Trouble*. Golden Press, Sydney, n.d..

Leckey, W.C. *Popular Mechanics How To Build Your Own Garage*. Popular Mechanics Press, Chicago, 1953.

'Leisure: He Does-It-Himself—and Then . . . He Collapses'. *Look*, 12 July 1955.

Lewis, P. (1978) *The Fifties: Portrait of an Age*. Herbert Press Ltd., London, 1989.

'Letterboxes: The Inside Story' (video). Australian Film Institute, South Melbourne, 1988.

'Living in a Garage'. *Australian Home Beautiful*, October 1958.

'Long Lost Brothers?' *People*, November 1991.

Lower, L. (1930) *Here's Luck*. Angus & Robertson Publishers, Sydney, 1980.

Maddock, J. *Mail for the Back of Beyond*. Kangaroo Press, Kenthurst, 1987.

'Mail of the Species'. *Good Weekend*, 4 August 1990.

'Mailboxes'. Standards Australia, DR 9412, 1994.

'Malcolm' (video). Cascade Films, Melbourne, 1986.

Maltin, L. (1980) *Of Mice and Magic: A History of American Animated Cartoons*. Plume, New York, 1987.

Mander, A.E. *The Making of the Australians*. Georgian House, Melbourne, 1958.

——. *6 p.m. Till Midnight*. Rawson's, Melbourne, 1945.

Manley, R. *Signs and Wonders: Outsider Art Inside North Carolina*. North Carolina Museum of Art, Raleigh, 1989.

Marcus, C.C. *Housing as if People Mattered*. University of California Press, Berkeley, 1986.

Marling, K.A. *As Seen on TV: The Visual Culture of Everyday Life in the 1950s*. Harvard University Press, Cambridge, 1994.

——. *The Colossus of Roads: Myth and Symbol Along the American Highway*. University of Minnesota Press, Minneapolis, 1984.

——. 'Disneyland, 1955: Just Take the Santa Ana Freeway to the American Dream'. *American Art*, Winter/Spring, 1991.

Marinetti, F.T. (1909). 'The Founding and Manifesto of Futurism' in Apollonio, U. (ed.), *Futurist Manifestos*. Thames & Hudson Ltd., London, 1973.

Maynard, J. *The Letterbox War of Kamarooka Street*. Bacon Town Books, Castlemaine, 1991.

McPherson's Guide for the Handyman. McPherson's Ltd., Melbourne, n.d..

'Meet Santa's Little Helper'. *Australasian Post*, 19 January 1991.

Mevissen, A. 'Letterbox Terror, Late Night Bombs Could Kill, Police'. *Sun*, 13 July 1990.

Mitchell, L. 'They're Building Their Own Home'. *Australian Home Beautiful*, March 1948.

Moore, C. et al. *The Place of Houses*. Holt, Rinehart & Winston, New York, 1974.

'Mrs Shepherd Is Not a Workshop Widow!' *Australian Home Beautiful*, August 1952.

Murray, R. 'You Can Become a Handy Handyman'. *Better Homes & Gardens*, June 1954.

'Now House & Garden Is On TV'. *Australian House & Garden*, July 1958.

Nunn, R. 'Handymen: Put Your Walls to Work Like This'. *Better Homes & Gardens*, October 1956.

——. 'Hollywood Handymen'. *Better Homes & Gardens*, November 1957.

——. 'The Thursday Night Club That Meets On Monday'. *Better Homes & Gardens*, December 1955.

O'Grady, J. (1957) *They're a Weird Mob*. Ure Smith Pty. Ltd., Sydney, 1965.

Olen, S. 'Spirit Houses'. *Mimar: Architecture in Development*, no. 38, March 1991.

Orr, R.H. 'Sculptural Advertising'. *Architect and Engineer*, vol. 91, October 1927.

Packard, V. (1957) *The Hidden Persuaders*. Penguin Books Ltd., Harmondsworth, 1961.

——. (1959) *The Status Seekers*. Penguin Books Ltd., Harmondsworth, 1961.

Papanek, V. (1972) *Design for the Real World: Human Ecology and Social Change*. Granada Publishing Ltd., Frogmore, 1974.

Pearce, C. *Fifties Source Book*. Chartwell Books, Secaucus, 1990.

Pearl, C. *So, You Want to Buy a House*. F.W. Cheshire Pty. Ltd., Melbourne, 1961.

Pennick, N. *Earth Harmony: Siting and Protecting Your Home, a Practical and Spiritual Guide*. Century Hutchinson Ltd., 1987.

Pevsner, N. (1943) An Outline of European Architecture. Penguin Books Ltd., Harmondsworth, 1977.

'Playhouse in the Summer Sun: You'll Be the Most Popular Dad in the Neighbourhood When You Build *This* House-O'-Fun!' *Science & Mechanics*, August 1963.

'Playhouse Is Fun, (A)'. *Australian House & Garden*, January 1951.

'Please Design Us a Dog Kennel'. *Australian Home Beautiful*, December 1957.

Plunkett, E.M. et al. 'Send Letters, Postcards, Drawings and Objects . . . The New York Correspondence School'. *Art Journal*, vol. 36, no. 3, Spring 1977.

Popular Mechanics Illustrated Home Handyman Encyclopedia & Guide, (The). J.J. Little & Ives Co. Inc., New York, 1961.

'Postbox Always Looks Nice, (The)'. *Good Weekend*, 23 June 1990.

'Postboxes . . . That Make It Easy for the Postman'. *Australian House & Garden*, September 1962.

Post Office Department Annual Reports, 1899. Post Office Department, Washington D.C., 1899.

Price, R. 'Post Taste'. *Australian Home Beautiful*, July 1948.

Pryor, D. 'Disneyland Down Under' in Belot, J., *Our Glorious Home*. Sun Books Pty. Ltd., South Melbourne, 1978.

Reid, M.H. *How to Use Portable Power Tools*. Thomas Y. Crowell Co., New York, 1954.

'Residential Premises', Australia Post, n.p., n.d..

Riley, T. 'Better Homes and Gardens Designs a Workshop'. *Better Homes & Gardens*, February 1959.

Ritter, B. 'Mailbox Artist'. *Profitable Hobbies*, February 1952.

Ross, H.E. & Walker, K.C. *Crash Tests of Rural Mailbox Installations*. Federal Highway Administration, Washington, 1980.

Russell, G. *Designer's Trade*. Allen & Unwin, London, 1968.

Rybczynski, W. *The Most Beautiful House in the World*. Viking, New York, 1989.

Rykwert, J. (1976) *The Idea of a Town: The Anthropology of Urban Form in Rome, Italy and the Ancient World*, MIT Press, Cambridge, 1988.

Scarry, R. (1968) *What Do People Do All Day?* William Collins Sons & Co. Ltd, Great Britain, 1987.

Schenk, W.P. (ed.). *1961 Popular Mechanics Workshop Annual* Popular Mechanics Co.. Chicago, 1961.

Schickel, R. *The Disney Version: The Life, Times, Art and Commerce of Walt Disney*. Simon & Schuster, New York, 1968.

Scuri, P. *Late-Twentieth-Century Skyscrapers*. Van Nostrand Reinhold, New York, 1990.

'Secure Living: A Victoria Police Guide'. Police Victoria, n.p., 1987.

Seddon, G. 'The Australian Backyard' in Phipps, J., *Backyards and Beyond*. State Library of Victoria, Melbourne, 1990.

Seney, N. 'If You Need Ideas, Here's the Shop'. *Better Homes & Gardens*, November 1959.

——. 'Planning Pays Off in This Workshop'. *Better Homes & Gardens*, November 1959.

Sexton, R. *American Style: Classic Product Design from Airstream to Zippo*. Chronicle Books, San Francisco, 1987.

Shepstone, H.J. 'In the Streets of Movieland' in Crossland, J.R. (ed.), *The Modern Marvels Encyclopedia*. Collins Clear-Type Press, London, n.d..

'Shop is Planned Around its Walls, (This)'. *Better Homes & Gardens*, December 1956.

Shute, N. *On the Beach*. William Heinemann Ltd., London, 1957.

——. *Trustee from the Toolroom*, Book Club, London, 1960.

Sibley, H. 'Mailboxes Can Be Made Attractive'. *Popular Mechanics What To Make and How To Make It*, vol. 10, Popular Mechanics Press, Chicago, 1949.

——. 'Ban Clutter from Your Workshop'. *Better Homes & Gardens*, April 1951.

Simmonds, R. 'How to Build a Small Power Saw'. *Australian Home Beautiful*, April 1946.

——. 'How to Make a Sanding Machine'. *Australian Home Beautiful*, July 1946.

SITE. *Highrise of Homes*. Rizzoli International Publications, Inc., New York, 1982.

Sixty Power Tools and How to Build Them. Popular Mechanics Co., Chicago, 1952.

Sloan, A. 'Letterbox Bomb Spree, Cat Killed in Random Attack'. *Herald Sun*, 28 March 1991.

Smith, A. *The Alex Smith Complete Home Furniture Maker Illustrated*. Colorgravure Publications, Melbourne, n.d..

——. *New Australian Home Carpentry Illustrated*. Colorgravure Publications, Melbourne, n.d..

——. *Australian Picture Handyman*. Heraldgrauve, Melbourne, n.d..

——. 'Carpentry for Women'. *Australian Home Beautiful*, February 1956.

——. 'How to Drive a Nail'. *Australian Home Beautiful*, February 1956.

——. 'Playhouse for the Children'. *Australian Home Beautiful*, December 1947.

——. 'Relax with a Leg-Rest'. *Australian Home Beautiful*, August 1956.

Smith, F.T. 'Equip Your Workshop with Power Tools: Take the Hard

Work out of Your Workshop by Mechanising It'. *Australian House and Garden*, November 1951.

Smith, K. *Ogf*. Ure Smith Pty. Ltd., Sydney, 1965.

Smithson, A. & P. (1956) 'But Today We Collect Ads' in Leffingwell, E. and Marta, K. (eds), *Modern Dreams: The Rise and Fall and Rise of Pop*. MIT Press, Cambridge, 1988.

Soule, G. 'House Planned for Workshopper'. *Popular Science Monthly*, April 1956.

Sowden, H. 'Harry Sowden on Living, Packaging and Dying', *Architecture in Australia*, vol. 63, no. 3, June 1974.

Spain, D. *Gendered Spaces*. University of North Carolina Press, Chapel Hill, 1992.

Spigel, L. *Make Room for TV: Television and the Family Ideal in Postwar America*. University of Chicago Press, Chicago, 1992.

Stewart, S. (1984) *On Longing: Narratives of the Miniature, the Gigantic, the Souvenir, the Collection*. Duke University Press, Durham, 1993.

Storrie, D. 'The Handyman'. *Australian Home Beautiful*, October 1953.

Stretton, H. *Housing and Government: 1974 Boyer Lectures by Hugh Stretton*. Australian Broadcasting Commission, Sydney, 1974.

Summerson, J. *Heavenly Mansions and Other Essays on Architecture*. Cresset Press Ltd., London, 1945.

'Systematic Remodelling: The Kitchen'. *Australian Handyman*, January 1950.

Taylor, J.P. '4 Do-It-Yourself Trends . . . That Mean Extra Profits to Advertisers'. *Printers' Ink*, 2 October 1953.

'They Came in All Shapes and Sizes'. *Australian Home Beautiful*, July 1968.

Thomson, M. *Blokes & Sheds*. Angus & Robertson, Pymble, 1995.

Tilton, G. (ed.) *Mechanix Illustrated How to Build It*. Fawcett Publications, Greenwich, 1951.

Townsend, H. *Baby Boomers: Growing Up in Australia in the 1940s, '50s and '60s*. Simon & Schuster Australia, Brookvale, 1988.

Tubbs, R. *The Englishman Builds*. Penguin Books Ltd., Harmondsworth, 1945.

van Oudtshoorn, N. & D. *Oddly Australian: An A to Z of the Weird, the Wonderful and the Oddball on the World's Biggest Island*. Bay Books, Kensington, 1984.

Vaughn, E. 'How to Put Your Tools Away'. *Better Homes & Gardens*, April 1955.

Venturi, R. (1966) *Complexity and Contradiction in Architecture*. Museum of Modern Art, New York, 1988.

Venturi, R. et al. (1972) *Learning from Las Vegas: The Forgotten Symbolism of Architectural Form*. MIT Press, Cambridge, 1988.

Vincent, C. 'Which Power Tools Shall I Buy?' *Australian Home Beautiful*, September 1948.

Walker, M. *Making Do: Memories of Australia's Back Country People*. Penguin Books Australia Ltd., Ringwood, 1982.

'Walt Disney: Teacher of Tomorrow'. *Look*, 17 April 1945.

Whitehead, L. 'When Will We All Have Homes?' *Australian Home Beautiful*, May 1948.

Weiss, G. & Leffingwell, E. 'The Necessity of Walls: The Impact of Television on Architecture' in Leffingwell, E. and Marta, K. (eds), *Modern Dreams: The Rise and Fall and Rise of Pop*. MIT Press, Cambridge, 1988.

'What a Whopper'. *Australasian Post*, 14 September 1991.

Wilde, M. (1989) *The Very Best of Friends*. Margaret Hamilton, Sydney, 1991.

Wilson, E. 'Which Power Tool Do You Need?' *Australian Home Beautiful*, August 1959.

Wilson, S. (1955) *The Man in the Grey Flannel Suit*. Paperjacks Ltd., Markham, 1985.

Wood, Mrs N. & Lapham, H. *Waiting for the Mail and Other Sketches and Poems*. George Robertson, Melbourne, 1875.

'You Can Put Up This Shelf'. *Practical Householder*, August 1958.

'You've Filled Our Letterbox!' *Australian Home Beautiful*, June 1968.

Zilliacus, L. (1956) *From Pillar to Post: The Troubled History of the Mail*. Heinemann Educational Books Ltd., London, 1963.

Index

Absent-minded Professor (The), 37
architecture,
    contemporary, 17
    gender, 18–19, 41, 48–50, 52–54, 57, 108
    models, 76–77, 83
    roadside, 19, 85–86, 88
Australia Post, 61, 69, 73, 88, 98
automation, 15, 31

Barrett, C., 65–66, 97, 98
'Better Homes & Gardens', 108
bird houses, 15
Bjorksten, M., 73
Black & Decker, 43, 44
Boyd, R., 9, 12, 16, 18, 19, 30
'Breakfast in Fur', 98
Breitgraf, H.J., 14
Breton, A., 63, 68
buildings, miniature, 54, 56, 75, 76–77, 83, 92, 97
'Burke's Backyard', 108

Carlyle, T., 42
cartoon characters, 37–38, 61, 71, 82, 90
cars, sexuality, 45–46, 48
ceremonial men's huts, 54
ceremonies, building, 12, 51, 74
City (The), 27
Cole, P.D., 97, 98
collage, 67–68, 106
computers, 73
Creeley, R., 51
Currie, B., 82

Danielson, A., 106
Dichter, E., 53–54
Dine, J., 45, 51
Disney, W., 32–33, 37, 54, 56, 57, 77, 83, 107
do-it-yourself, popularity, 18, 23, 107

products, 14–15, 23
projects, 15, 39
publications, 14, 23, 24, 25, 26, 29, 30, 32, 34, 35, 36, 37, 43, 44, 45, 47, 49, 50, 55–56, 57, 62, 91, 92
television, 24–25, 35–36, 73, 107
tradesmen, 24, 28, 86
do-it-yourselfers,
    backyard inventors, 36–38
    executives, 32–33
    female, 26, 35, 38, 45, 47, 108
    handymen, hopeless, 18, 25, 33–36, 37, 38, 52
    male, 18, 25, 26, 32, 35, 38, 41, 108
    movie stars, 47–48
    owner-builders, 14, 18, 23, 27–28, 29
doghouses, 15, 30
dolls' houses, 12, 54, 55, 97
Duchamp, M., 98

e-mail, 64, 72, 108
Edna Everage (Dame), 63
efficiency, 48–50, 51
Egar, A., 14
Evans, D., 105

fallout shelters, 57
faxes, 72, 108
featurism, 30
feng-shui, 12
'Five Feet of Colourful Tools', 51
Flank Breeder, 82
flying saucers, 57
folk art, 19, 67, 88, 89, 91, 95, 107, 108
'Fountain', 98

garages, live-in, 28
garden ornaments, 15, 30

Gilbert, C., 76
Gilbreth, F. & L., 48, 49
Graham, D., 72–73
Graham, J., 97–99
Graves, M., 91
gravestones, 99–100

Hardy, M., 26
'Healthy, Wealthy & Wise', 108
Henderson, N., 57
'Highrise of Letterboxes', 74–75
'Home Improvement', 35–36
'House & Garden Magazine Show', 25
housing, highrise, 74–75
    modern, 17, 29–30
    shortage, 14, 27
    styles, 16–17
Huzairi, A., 106

isolation, Australia, 16
    women, 52–53

job satisfaction, 31
Johnson, P., 77
Jones, C. & E., 27–28
Joroleman, R., 89

kitchens, 48–50

labour, shortage, 14
Lam, J., 106
Lee, M., 53
Leicester, A., 45, 77
leisure, 31, 36
letterboxes,
    animals, 61, 62, 67, 71, 80, 83, 86, 87, 88, 91, 94, 95, 98–100, 108
    boundary markers, 15–16, 69, 83, 96, 98, 99–100
    buildings, 18, 62, 82–83, 92, 94, 95, 97
    bush, 61, 64–67, 98

creativity, 15, 19, 37, 67–68, 93, 108
crimes, 19, 77–79, 93
education, 13, 19, 94–97
exhibitions, 12, 19, 89, 97–107
fire alarms, 12, 13, 78, 84
fire extinguishers, 13, 84
fire hydrants, 13, 61, 84
guardians, 19, 69, 80–84, 93, 99, 100–101, 104, 108
history, 16–18, 38, 61, 89
hobbies, 19, 69, 81, 87, 95
home, symbol of, 16, 19, 73–77, 78, 90, 93, 108
houses, 12, 16, 18, 30, 37, 61, 62, 75–76, 88, 91, 94, 95, 102, 108
location, 13, 19, 61, 62, 69, 77–78, 79, 80
mail, 16, 71–72, 78, 92–93, 94, 97, 101–103, 104, 105
making, 14, 15, 18, 19, 38, 57, 93, 94–95, 96, 97, 98
Ned Kelly, 62, 81, 94
occupations, 19, 68, 69, 86–87, 93, 97
people, 61, 62, 81–82, 83, 92, 94, 100–101, 105, 106
place, symbol of, 14, 19, 61, 62, 69–71, 75, 87, 88, 90–91, 95, 97, 98–99, 104
recycling, 12, 15, 30, 61, 62–63, 64–68, 71–72, 76, 86, 88, 89, 92, 94, 95, 96, 102, 103–104, 106, 108
self, symbol of, 14, 67, 70–71, 92, 95, 97–98, 99–100, 101–102, 104, 108
sizes, 89
snails, 63–64
standardisation, 19, 89
statistics, 61, 73
suburban, 12, 14, 17–18, 62, 67, 90
trees, 12, 62, 65, 92
United States, 14, 19, 30, 89–92

vehicles, 16, 37, 61, 62, 68, 86, 88, 91, 92, 95
weapons, 13, 61, 62, 83
Lovett, L., 97, 100
Lueckenhausen, H., 97, 99–100

'Machine Dedicated to Spike Jones', 36
mail art, 68, 105–107
Malcolm, 37
Marinetti, F.T., 48
materials, building, 23
shortage, 14, 29
Maynard, J., 17–18
McCormick, M., 97, 100–101

'Nature Teaches Us the Importance of Living', 103
Newsome, M., 97, 100–101
Nino Culotta, 27
'Nouveau Rat Trap', 36
nuclear power, 56–57
Nunneley, J.S., 106

Oakes, R.E., 36
Oppenheim, M., 98

Paolozzi, E., 57
'Patio and Pavilion', 57
pegboard, 51
pioneers, suburban, 28, 90
playhouses, 54–56
postmen (posties), 13, 14, 66, 71, 89, 97, 100, 106
'Prospect V-II', 45

Ray, M., 98
Reed, A., 97, 102
Riskin, R., 106
Ross, D., 106
Rowe, P., 95–96

Sandy Stone, 63
Scaramuzzino, J., 96
Selenitsch, A., 97, 102–103
Sherlock Holmes, 9–10, 11–12, 107
Shopsmith, 26, 43
Smith, A., 24, 35, 56
Smith, J., 97, 102
Smithson, A. & P., 57, 107
Snow White and the Seven Dwarfs, 54

speed, 45–46, 48
spirit houses, 83
Stahle, R., 29
stamps, postage, 68, 105
rubber, 105
Stephens, S., 106
stress, 32
surrealism, 63, 68–69, 98

Takizawa, A., 97, 102–103
talismans, Chinese, 12–13, 80, 84
Western, 80, 84
'Three Fridges', 66
Thursday Night Club, 26, 44
Tigerman, S., 91
togetherness, 52, 53
tools, care, 43
hand, 41, 42–43, 45, 50–51
power, 15, 23, 24, 26, 32, 41, 43–45, 46–48, 53, 108
sexuality, 46–47
storage, 41, 50–52, 54

Venturi, R., 30, 77, 85, 88, 91
'Video Projection Outside Home', 73
'Violon d'Ingres (Le)', 98

'Walt's Workshop', 25
Watts, M. & B., 79
Westermann, H.C., 36–37, 45
'Where the Mail Goes Cream of Wheat Goes', 89
Wild One (The), 31
Wong, D., 97, 103–104
work, 15, 31–32
workshops, home, 18–19, 23, 36, 39–42, 49, 53
fallout shelters, 18, 57
flying saucers, 57
kitchens, 49–50, 57, 108
location, 19, 39–40, 41
male sanctums, 18, 52–54, 57, 107
playhouses, 18, 55–56, 57
statistics, 23
storage, 41, 49, 50–52
workplace, 18
Wyeth, N., 89

yard shrines, 83